Restoring the Mind of Black America

Dr. Eddie Taylor

African American Images
Chicago, IL

Front cover illustration by Harold Carr

ISBN #: 1-934155-61-6
ISBN #: 978-1-934155-61-5

Contents

Acknowledgments

Nothing in life can be accomplished or have meaning without the help of other people. A multitude of people supported me throughout the journey of writing this book.

Thanks to Dr. Avedis Panajian for giving me the inspiration to write about this topic. His lectures were very informative, and his understanding of the many aspects of psychological reparation and restoration of the mind was extremely helpful. Thanks to Dr. Christine Lewis for her timely response and direction regarding my early manuscripts. Her feedback and suggestions motivated me to make repeated trips to the library. Thanks to Dr. George Didier for working with me, supporting me, and generously sharing his various psychological perspectives with me.

Thanks to Solomon, Loretta, Malik, Kareema, Latifah, Leroy, Syrus, and Joseph, the participants in this study who shared their life experiences and thoughts about the restoration of the African American community. (Their names have been changed to protect their privacy.) Their openness and candor were like gold to the alchemist.

Many thanks to the following important people: my mother, Lillie Robinson; brother, Ulyess Taylor, Jr.; sisters Brenda, Gailynn, Pamela, and Kimberlerine—as well as my friends and colleagues who encouraged and supported me.

To everyone who gave of their time, provided a word of encouragement, shared some advice, suggested a book or an article, or prayed for me, I am truly grateful.

Finally, I thank my wife, Jesseann Taylor, for her support and understanding spirit throughout this entire process. Thanks also to my children, Eddie, Jr., Evan, and Jameka, who listen to my ideas.

Introduction: Remains of the Revolution

As an African American, I have been inspired by the triumphs of the Civil Rights Movement. The messages and purpose of the movement have renewed my sense of identity and self-respect. Having grown up in the inner city, however, I have been perplexed to witness violence, hatred, and crime. How could such a powerful movement disintegrate into such terrible social decline in virtually every area of African American life? My calling, and the purpose of this book, is to document and understand the decline of the African American community that has occurred since the end of the Civil Rights Movement.

The pain within the African American community can be traced back to slavery. After the abolition of slavery and the end of the Civil War, the U.S. government attempted to assimilate the freed Africans into American society during the Reconstruction Era.

In 1865, Black Southerners staked their claims to becoming a free people and to enjoying the fruits of freedom. They began to project a very different vision of the future than they and their parents had known. During slavery, freedom for some had been impossible to contemplate. Now they aspired to a better life. They wanted what only Whites had enjoyed—the vote, education, freedom to worship, freedom to marry legally, judicial equity, and the chance to not only work on their own plots of land but to retain the rewards of their labor. During Reconstruction, they seized the opportunity to make these goals a reality. They were determined to reorder the post-bellum South. It was a time of unparalleled hope, laden with possibility, when Black men and women took action to shape their own destiny (Litwack, 1998, p. xiii).

By the early 1870s, Blacks had won hundreds of political offices. Some officeholders from both the North and South were already free; others were former slaves who had served in the Union Army. Many could read and write. A few Black candidates decided to enter the political arena; they were elected as United States senators and representatives, lieutenant governors, state treasurers, superintendents of education, and state legislators (Wormser, 2003, p. 27).

The goal of Jim Crow[1] laws was to halt Black progress. They created a renewed sense of inferiority and degradation within the Black community. Jim Crow was not merely about the physical separation of Blacks and Whites. Nor was segregation strictly about laws, despite historians' tendency to fixate upon such legal landmarks as *Plessy v. Ferguson* (1896), *Brown v. Board of Education* (1954), and the Civil Rights Act of 1964. Whites needed more than signs that specified "Whites Only" and "Blacks Only" to maintain their dominant status; they had to assert and reiterate Black inferiority with every law, word, and gesture in every aspect of both public and private life (Chafe, et al., 2001, p. 1).

Jim Crow laws reduced African Americans to standards far below equal human rights and dignity. The laws made no exception regarding class or education. Indeed, they functioned on one level: to remind Black people that no matter how educated, wealthy, or respectable they might be, they would never be entitled to equal treatment with the poorest and most degraded Whites (Litwack, 1998, p. 238).

The Jim Crow era began with the infamous Compromise of 1877. Republican politicians sold out Black Americans when they agreed to remove Federal troops that had been stationed in the South to enforce Reconstruction. In return, they received electoral commission votes for their candidate, Rutherford B. Hayes, in the disputed Tilden-Hayes presidential election of 1876. From that point on, the "equal protections" supposedly guaranteed to Black citizens under the Fourteenth

Introduction: Remains of the Revolution

Amendment disappeared in practice. Systematic disenfranchisement began in the 1890s with the imposition of Jim Crow segregation statutes that were ultimately sanctioned by the U.S. Supreme Court in the *Plessy v. Ferguson* case of 1896 (Litwack, pp. xxv–xxvi).

The Unifying Movement

As I studied the historical rollercoaster of my people, I noticed that the Civil Rights Movement unified the community and instilled a new consciousness. Although problems existed within the community, the dominant theme was unity. I was not actively involved in the movement; however, the movement ameliorated my understanding of who I am and how significant it is for any group of people to work together for a common goal. The Civil Rights Movement uplifted the African American community and brought international awareness to our struggle in America. Unfortunately, since the assassinations of key leaders, the demise of our community into a maladaptive existence has been transmitted through mass media and the Internet to every corner of the globe.

In this study, I will endeavor to understand the purpose and direction of the Civil Rights Movement through its leaders, primarily Dr. Martin Luther King, Jr., Malcolm X, and the Black Panther Party. We will also look at the community's deep-rooted psychological pain caused in part by the abrupt end of the Civil Rights Movement.

My community has been inflicted with crime, degradation, division, self-hatred, and many other problems. Many laws have been passed to ameliorate our condition, but internally something is missing. Internally, we have been severely wounded. I have witnessed minority groups rising from "nobodies" to become "somebodies" while my own community remains complacent and in a depressed state. No matter where you go in America, our people barely exist in the worst parts of major cities. This saddens me deeply.

Yet despite the many obstacles, we have made progress. We are a resilient people. Much was achieved during the Civil Rights Movement. We were Black and Proud and Black and Beautiful. To gain awareness and self-identity, the African American community as a whole began to revisit slavery. We marched together, boycotted together, and struggled together.

In the 1950s, the Civil Rights Movement began to gain momentum. From its subtle beginnings during the Harlem Renaissance to its violent climax in the South, the Civil Rights Movement provided the Black community with direction, guidance, and hope for a better life in America. It gave us an American identity and purpose. The movement transformed a despised community into one willing to die for equality as American citizens. The leaders of the movement created a new consciousness for Blacks, one that fused together our ancient African connection, the pain of slavery, and the promise of freedom. Refusing to conform to the status quo of discrimination, racism, and inequality, civil rights leaders created hope in the midst of despair, self-worth within a nation of neglect, and a spirit of brotherhood in a world of hate. The Civil Rights Movement gave birth to a new group of Americans—Black Americans. Realizing what was lost through slavery, the Black community accepted for the moment that America was home.

The community did not ask for pity or handouts. Rather, we were committed to using our talents, skills, and vision to transform this nation into a beacon to the world.

Unfortunately, the Civil Rights Movement ended abruptly after the assassination of our leaders and the co-opting of our institutions, and the community was left in chaos. We began to exist in total opposition to our purpose. All values, morals, and principles that once existed within the community began to fade away. Internally we began to implode. The drug abuse that is running rampant throughout the community is not a drug problem. Illegal drugs are being used in a misguided attempt to bear the seemingly unbearable pain of reality.

The community has been without courageous leadership or an organized platform for too long. It appears we are no longer willing to fight for equality and justice.

The topic for this study, the psychological destruction of the African American community and the need for healing, came to me while I was an undergraduate student in Texas. A course I had taken on African American history heightened my awareness of how hated and despised we are in America. I began to remember experiences I endured during my childhood.

This is how consciousness is raised. For example, during the mid-1900s, African American educators studied African history. They glimpsed an ancient past that had been stolen from us during slavery. This legacy connected us to a larger existence, one that stretched beyond the difficulties of America to the Motherland, Africa. We struggled with how to be both African and American.

Research Methodology

Methodology is all-important in research. When trying to understand a phenomenon, a researcher will select what he believes to be the best method for studying the unknown. The protocols, instruments, etc. of the method must be rigorous enough to provide a reliable window into the soul of the problem. A way of communicating the problem, process, results, and healing value of the study will emerge through the methodology. That which has been concealed will become visible with the right methodology.

Any study that addresses the hearts and behaviors of men, women, and children must embrace the soul. As James Hillman (1983) stated, "Our way...does not interpret the image but talks with it" (p. 93). Hillman uses the term "image" to describe the psyche, or the soul. When a therapist talks with the image/soul of an individual, knowledge is gained.

The research was time consuming and financially demanding. The participants in this work were selected based upon their involvement with the Civil Rights Movement or their involvement within the African American community. The scope of work included an extensive literature review and field interviews. Areas of study included the following:

1. Literature review of psychological and social reparation.
2. Literature review of the Civil Rights Movement.
3. In-depth interviews with eight community activists. The interviews were taped and transcribed.

Psychological and Social Reparation

Why, after so much progress, did we simply give up? Why weren't we able to rebound after the loss of our leaders? In life we grieve and then move on. But the community as a whole has been unable to pick up where Dr. King, Malcolm X, and the Black Panther Party left off. We are still suffering from this loss, and this in part explains the disproportionate rates of substance abuse, fatherlessness, academic failure, poverty, and incarceration in the African American community.

This study is about our dull, unconscious pain. When we lost our beloved leaders, instead of properly grieving as a community, our unconsciousness within the community erected defense mechanisms that attempted to block the pain. As a result, the pain has not been properly experienced in our souls. We will never be healed if we do not process through the pain. Slavery was one cause of the pain; however, in this book I will discuss the opening of the wound that occurred at the end of the Civil Rights Movement. Just when we were on the threshold of true progress, our leaders and organizations were killed, disappeared, or became ineffective.

This study will consist of two distinct forms of communal healing: *psychological reparation*, as defined by R. D.

Introduction: Remains of the Revolution

Hinshelwood (1991) and Melanie Klein (1940, 1964), and *social reparations*, as defined by the Reparations Coordinating Committee (RCC) and bill H.R. 40, the Commission to Study Reparation Proposals for African Americans Act, introduced by Congressman John Conyers in January 1989 (Haley, 2004).

Psychological reparation. Klein's theory offers a way to understand the anger, violence, and loss of direction that have taken root in our community since the end of the Civil Rights Movement. This theory looks at how we face pain and avoid pain, how the urge to repair damage done to others develops and how this urge is denied unconsciously. We face pain through the psychological process of "reparation"; through this experience of suffering we grow and *repair* ourselves and our community. This process occurs through the *depressive position*, more commonly known as guilt, anger, aggression, etc. Processing through these seemingly negative emotions will enable us ultimately to grow and develop more effectively as a community.

On the other hand, we *avoid* pain (and consequently healing) through the psychological process of "manic reparation"; engaging in behaviors such as crime, substance abuse, and violence means that we are unable to perceive the pain and suffering of others. These behaviors, or defenses, appear as *paranoid-schizoid mechanisms*, i.e., psychological implosions and fragmentation resulting in addictions, violence, crime, academic failure, etc. Without the ability to process and experience the negative emotions, we become trapped and are unable to connect to reality.

What does Klein's theory mean within the context of the Black community? During the Civil Rights Movement, we were unified and steadily moving toward progress. Today we are in complete denial of our collective pain, and as a result, we have erected unconscious defense mechanisms, such as guilt, shame, and rage, that have led to destructive behaviors against self and others. If we don't process through these emotions, we remain unaware of the suffering of our brothers and sisters in the African American community.

Social reparations. Social reparations, as defined by the RCC, began in the 1800s after the Emancipation Proclamation ended slavery in the United States. The goal was to repair the socio-economic damage by granting to the former slaves and their descendants real estate, land, money, and livestock.

The nearest the U.S. government came to fulfilling its promise was when Union commanders, empowered by General William Sherman's Field Order 15 of January 1865, made land grants and provided other material assistance to the newly liberated Blacks. However, that order was rescinded by President Andrew Johnson later in the year. Efforts by Representative Thaddeus Stevens and other radical Republicans to provide the proverbial 40 acres and a mule that would have carved up huge plantations of the defeated Confederacy into modest land grants for Blacks never came to fruition. To date, the debt has not been paid (Haley, 2004, pp. 20–21).

The issue of economic reparations has concerned African Americans since the 1800s, post-bellum. Attempts to secure reparations were made through political efforts immediately following the Civil War. Today Randall Robinson (2002), William Banks (2001), Congressman John Conyers, Jr., and others continue to advocate for economic reparations.

Two Spellings

Throughout this study you'll note two different spellings for the word *reparation.* When used in connection with economic and political restitution, the spelling is *reparations* (plural). I will defer to John Torpey's (2006) definitions:

> "...reparation is more akin to the idea of restoration of the state of affairs before the violation occurred. By contrast, reparations

have come to be used almost synonymously with compensation—that is, with money transfers of a relatively direct kind. One *makes* reparation, in short, but one *pays* reparations." (p. 45)

Torpey says that "the singular of the term connotes a multiplicity of activities." For our purposes, the most important activity is psychological reparation.

The Hope

We may try to avoid acknowledging the pain and loss, but we will never forget the annihilation of our leaders. We have not forgotten the symbol of hope our leaders embodied. These are the psychic ambiguities we live with on a daily basis and that undermine the repair and integration of our souls.

Contrary to popular opinion, the problems that exist in our community are not innate to African Americans. Violence is not our natural state of being. It is not normal for us to engage in such self-destructive behaviors. It is my sincere desire that the readers of this book will embark upon their own healing journey toward sanity and wholeness. We must remember the voices of our leaders, understand the essence of our psychological symptoms, and begin to move toward a renewed reality. Only then will we begin to heal as a community.

"A Different Image"

The age requires this task:
create a different image;
re-animate the mask.
Shatter the icons of slavery and fear.
Replace the leer of the minstrel's burnt-cork face
with a proud, serene and classic
bronze of Benin. (Randall, 1968, p. 142)

Part 1: Framework

Chapter 1: Research Philosophy

As a researcher and an African American man, I want to thoroughly understand how a movement that gave me hope, identity, and empowerment devolved into pain and agony. A plethora of maladaptive behaviors emerged out of the Civil Rights Movement. This topic moves me emotionally and keeps me up at night.

The African way is to have a tribal leader or chief give direction to the people. Today, African Americans are suspicious of leaders, and we fear becoming leaders. I want to understand how this phenomenon is connected to the death of the Civil Rights Movement, a movement that saw its unfair share of death and tragedy.

Black street gangs have been studied to understand how and why they exist, but I want to understand how street gangs emerged out of the Civil Rights Movement. Gangs are more than "family" for the members. They generate wealth in the underground economy, to the harm and sorrow of all involved. How did our Black organizations degenerate into destructiveness?

I want to understand the pain that has led to violence in my community. This type and breadth of violence did not exist until the post-civil rights era.

Despite all the studies, targeted legislation, conferences, books, workshops, university courses, panel discussions, and documentaries, the pain continues. I believe a phenomenological approach will help us understand.

According to David Stewart (1974), phenomenology is "a reasoned inquiry which discovers the inherent essences of appearances…an appearance is anything of which one is conscious" (p. 3). Consciousness is vital to phenomenology. The recognition and meaning of an experience are founded upon an individual being conscious. "Both phenomenology and psychology are concerned with consciousness in general as well as specific acts of consciousness such as perception, memory, comprehension of meaning, reasoning, etc." (Gurwitsch, 1966, p. 89).

Stewart (1974) concludes that quantitative methods are inadequate in a phenomenological approach. Phenomenology is not an objective method because consciousness is not an object. Thus a more subjective, qualitative approach is required.

Edmund Gustav Albrecht Husserl, Georg Hegel, and Martin Heidegger are among the notable philosophers of phenomenology. "Edmund Husserl, the motive force in the development of phenomenology, has remained the philosophic mentor to subsequent phenomenologists" (Stewart, 1974, p. 15).

The phenomenological approach to philosophical inquiry includes phenomenological reduction, phenomenological epoch, and bracketing.

> "*The Phenomenological Reduction.* It is a common mode of expression to speak of reducing a complex problem to its basic elements. This reduction involves a narrowing of attention to what is essential in the problem while disregarding or ignoring the superfluous and accidental. What one ignores when performing the phenomenological reduction is his previous prejudice about the world. By narrowing his attention to what is essential, he hopefully will discover the rational principles necessary for an understanding of the thing (or phenomenon) under investigation.
>
> "*The Phenomenological Epoche.* This narrowing of attention involves the suspension of certain commonly held beliefs. To describe this aspect of the shift from the natural to the

philosophical attitude, Husserl used the Greek term *epoche,* which was a technical term used by the Greek skeptics to refer to a suspension of judgment.

"*Bracketing.* Being a mathematician, Husserl also referred to the phenomenological reduction as placing the natural attitude toward the world in brackets .... In mathematics, one brackets (or parenthesizes) a mathematical equation in order to treat it differently. By bracketing the equation, the mathematician does not eliminate it, but merely places it out of question for the present, while the larger context of the equation is investigated." (Stewart, 1974, p. 26)

The phenomenological method promotes direct experience over secondhand knowledge (obtained from books or hearsay, for example).

"William A. Luijpen (1966) illustrates an example of phenomenology: How is it that I learn the meaning of landscapes, rivers and seas? Is it really through books on geography that I gain this meaning? Whoever proposes such a solution fools himself. It is true that a book on geography contains worthwhile scientific knowledge pertaining to landscapes, seas and rivers, but this knowledge is accessible to me only on the basis of a more fundamental and absolutely original experience; this experience comprises our every day spontaneous contact with landscapes, seas and rivers." (Stewart, 1974, p. 9)

Thus, phenomenology searches for truth based solely on an individual's personal experiences in his world. Husserl "continues to see phenomenology as a method that will lead us to the indisputable by way of a return to the *things themselves*…. Only when experience is viewed in this way can it serve as a foundation upon which all true statements can securely rest" (p. 21). Phenomenology, then, seeks to reveal the innermost truth beyond philosophical assumptions or empirical methodologies.

> "Phenomenology when seen as an endeavor to uncover the foundations of philosophy, when seen as a method by means of which we can reach the indisputable ground of truth, needs to unmask all philosophical prejudices concerning the nature of consciousness. This unmasking brings in its wake the reinstatement of actual experience as it is lived, namely, as presence to and uncovering of the *lived-world*." (p. 22)

Meaning is the most important aspect of experience. Whether an experience is meaningful or meaningless determines whether things change or remain the same. "An individual approaches the life world with a *stock of knowledge* composed of common sense constructs and categories that are social in origin. These images, theories, ideas, values, and attitudes are applied to aspects of experience, making them meaningful" (Denzin and Lincoln, 1998, p. 139).

Phenomenology is not concerned with scientific or quantitative findings. I felt it was of utmost importance to select interviewees who had direct experience of the issues being examined. Only their experiences could give meaning to the topic. This method allowed the participants to freely communicate their opinions and experiences in their own

Chapter 1: Research Philosophy

unique ways. Although I believe that with more understanding we'll begin to heal, the objective was not to find a cure *per se*; rather, it was to honor the experiences of the participants.

> "It may be neither necessary nor sufficient for predicting a person's behavior to know about his phenomenal perspective and feelings. But it certainly adds substantially to a full understanding of his conduct, and is in this sense relevant." (Lee and Mandelbaum, 1967, p. 223)

During the interviews, it was important to establish a safe, trusting, emotional bond so that the participants felt free to disclose personal experiences. The phenomenological method allowed the participants' statements to be heard, free from my own personal biases. As the experts and authority of their experiences, the interviewees assumed the role of the "wise old man," which helped to establish trust. Hopefully, by peering into the conscious and unconscious realities of those who live and work in the trenches of the African American community, this study will enhance meaning for us all— including those nations in the Middle East that are currently demanding their own civil rights.

How can a phenomenological approach help us to better understand the destruction that occurred in the Black community immediately following the Civil Rights Movement? A phenomenological approach will allow those who are familiar with the movement and those who lived through it to tell their stories in their own way. The participants are not objects to be observed. They are human beings to be engaged. In this approach, researcher and participants interact as peers on equal ground.

If there is a shortcoming to this approach it is that there is no objectivity at all. All participants were involved, are currently involved, or have a vested interested in the Civil Rights Movement. Those who experienced the movement firsthand aren't always able to articulate their experiences. It may be difficult locating researchers who are on both sides of the movement: the progressive and the condescending aspects of the struggle. Some may choose not to recall or express their experiences. Also, the ability to validate this qualitative approach is more challenging than with quantitative or empirical research.

It is my sincere desire that those who have been touched, either directly or indirectly, by the negative behaviors and conditions in the Black community will find this study cathartic.

Chapter 2: Psychological Reparation

In this study we will be taking the liberty of applying psychoanalysis to the African American community as a whole. Psychological reparation within the African American community involves a psychoanalytic approach to the community's experience. As such, the African American community is represented by the child; the leaders and organizations are the mother or primary internalized loved object.[2] This chapter will demonstrate how the loss of the civil rights leaders and organizations (primary loved objects) has affected the community psychologically from the Kleinian perspective.

Psychoanalytic theory was developed by observing and analyzing patients of non-African heritage. The pioneering theorists were neither African nor American. Whereas it is likely that some of their constituents were victims of colonization, hatred, and discrimination, they were able to identify a legitimate association with their own people. Since this is not the case with the African American community, I will employ the principles of psychoanalysis with the assumption that "most," not all, things are equal. The work of Melanie Klein and others should not be disregarded, but given the demographics of their patients, we can imagine why the African American community has not thoroughly embraced the idea of analysis.

Contributions for this section are from the following: Michael St. Clair (2000), Bernard Brandchaft (1986), James Astor (2002), H. Solomon (1991), J. Craig Peery (2002), Sigmund Freud (1914, 1917, 1995), Joseph Sandler (2003), Ernest Jones (1953), Paul Roazen (1974), Melanie Klein (1935, 1940, 1943), R. D. Hinshelwood (1991), A. A. Mason (1977), Meira Likierman (2001), Otto Fenichel (1943), B. Burch (1989), Hanna Segal (1964), John Steiner (1992), Judith Edwards (2005), Herbert Rosenfeld (1959), Neil Altman (2005), and Joan Riviere (Klein and Riviere, 1964).

Restoring the Mind of Black America

Sigmund Freud and Psychoanalysis

Sigmund Freud was the father of psychoanalysis. His great contribution to the field of mental health was his discovery of the importance of the unconscious—its role in human behavior and the use of clinical psychoanalysis to uncover unconscious motivations for behavior. Freud's book, *The History of the Psychoanalytic Movement* (1914/1995), explains his theory.

> "For psychoanalysis is my creation; for ten years I was the only one occupied with it, and all the annoyance which this new subject caused among my contemporaries has been hurled upon my head in the form of criticism. Even today, when I am no longer the only psychoanalyst, I feel myself justified in assuming that nobody knows better than I what psychoanalysis is, wherein it differs from other method of investigating the psychic life, what its name should cover, or what might better be designated as something else." (p. 901)

Freud's investigations and clinical practice "taught him that the most complicated processes of thought could go on without being accompanied by consciousness, and he habitually referred to these as 'unconscious mental processes' " (Jones, 1953, p. 368). Freud postulated the independence of the unconscious; I also maintain that the unconscious operates and exists autonomously. My study of the African American community is rooted in psychoanalytic theory and the unconscious.

Object Relations Theory

This writing focuses on one of the important streams of psychoanalytic thought: object relations theory (St. Clair,

Chapter 2: Psychological Reparation

2000, p. xiii). "Object relations, broadly speaking, refers to an internal and external world of relationships. Object is a technical term referring to 'that which a subject relates.' Discussions of object relations usually center on the early relations of a child and mother and how this early relationship shapes the child's inner world and later adult relationships" (St. Clair, p. xiii).

To apply an object relations perspective to the African American community requires some modifications of the theory. Sigmund Freud's theory of object relations misses the point of this study, for he had little concern with the soul or deeper aspects of relationships. "He used *instinct* to explain the relationships and environmental forces that shape an individual's personality. The instincts serve as the framework for his discussions of motivation and object relationships. He assumed that biological or instinctual drives are primary and precede the object" (St. Clair, 2000, p. 22). The object relations concentration for the African American community has little if anything to do with instinctual drives, unless one could equate nationality and instincts, which one would be hard pressed to do. Freud's object was a more literal object than that which Melanie Klein and other theorists presumed. "When Freud looked at an individual's current behavior in terms of a past relationship with a significant person, he saw the relationship's significance in terms of the role that person played in arousing or satisfying the individual's needs rather than who or what that person was" (St. Clair, p. 22).

Regardless of Freud's emphasis on drives and instincts, his theory of object relations was pregnant with new ideas about the unconscious. "Object relations theory could be thought to have begun when Freud and his followers were forced to pay more and more attention to transference phenomena and when Freud decided that reports from his patients of early childhood sexual abuse were the result of fantasies and not of reality" (Solomon, 1991, p. 316).

Restoring the Mind of Black America

The theory of object relations held a primary role within the psychoanalytic community.

> "In the 1930s object relations became the major focus for the school of psychoanalysis developed particularly in London. Melanie Klein came to England before the war in order to establish a base for her own investigations into early infantile life, the results of which were to radically question some of Freud's basis tenets. She developed a method of observation with her play technique, and, from her observations, the bases of object relations theory were conceived. The two important aspects of internal objects that concern us here are 1) that they are mental representations of instincts, and 2) that they are given their particular shape by internalizing the experience of a real object, which modifies the original mental representation." (Solomon, 1991, p. 317)

Klein's theory provides a way of looking into the unconscious of the African American community through its internalization of certain loved objects (leaders and organizations). Thus, what was experienced externally has become internalized. It is this internalization of a real object that moves from a drive or instinct in Freud's theory to a more personal and phenomenal relationship. Solomon (1991) does a good job of illustrating Freud's influence on the psychoanalytic developments of Melanie Klein and her insights into how external objects are internalized in the unconscious. From there, Klein postulated that internalized loved objects were genuine, legitimate, nurturing people.

Chapter 2: Psychological Reparation

Solomon (1991) quoted Klein's perception of the infant's awareness of the mother prior to birth. He said that Klein's acknowledgement of an instinctual relationship between mother and infant "exemplifies Klein's idea of the internal object which pre-exists the experience of the real mother but which will be mediated by the experience of the real mother" (p. 319).

Psychological Reparation and Manic Reparation

Freud's ideas laid the foundation for many who followed him, and that included Melanie Klein. She was a contemporary of Freud, but they had only a "slight personal relationship" (Roazen, 1974, p. 478). However, he did influence her thinking to a great degree. "Klein's stress on the role of inner fantasies was only an extension of Freud's own position; but, for her, unconscious fantasies (internal objects) became the crux of human life, both normal as well as pathological. Regression in the course of therapy becomes then not a danger signal but a sign of the deepening of an analysis" (p. 482).

Although reparation was introduced to the psychoanalytical community by Melanie Klein, ironically, reparation was not the initial theory that Klein sought to establish. She is regarded as one of the foremost pioneers of child psychoanalysis.

Klein began her career as a child psychoanalyst in 1919. Her work was revolutionary in that she worked with children six years old and younger. In "The Psychological Principles of Infant Analysis" (1986), Klein refers to some of the children she treated: "The analysis of one child of two years and nine months, another of three years and a quarter, and several children of about four years old" (p. 59). Through her work with children, she discovered psychological reparation—a process that could be used to treat both children and adults.

Psychological reparation. Klein believed that when loss or damage occurred to a patient's internalized loved object (a mother or father figure, for example), psychological reparation (repair) was required to bring health and wholeness to the individual. In the case of the African American community, the lost and damaged loved objects are our assassinated leaders and dismantled organizations. Only when we, the African American community, begin to acknowledge the damage and loss on a deep, emotional, soul level can the process of healing begin. The inner drive toward reparation is as strong as the sexual libido (Klein and Riviere, 1964).

Manic reparation. Where reparation is the process of mental and emotional healing, manic reparation is the opposite. In fact, *manic* is derived from *mania*. The goal of manic reparation is to avoid, at all cost, feelings of guilt and loss. To do this, the ego erects defenses to prevent the individual from experiencing guilt and loss. In the community, violence is one such defense, but of course, this only leads to more guilt and loss. It's a vicious cycle. To understand Klein is to understand these two opposing forces—the drive to be mature, whole, and emotionally healthy (reparation) and the drive to plunge our self-absorbed, fearful heads into the sands of avoidance (manic reparation).

Hinshelwood (1991) explains that manic reparation occurs when the internalized loved object is considered beyond repair.

> "The anguish of wanting to repair so totally damaged an object stems from the fact that this is experienced as a vastly demanding task. As a result the whole situation has to be belittled and the task made light of, as if it can be accomplished by magic.
>
> Later in life even normal stresses can provoke the contemptuous phantasy that anyway the object is not worth bothering about. But the contempt and belittling are manic defenses against the severity of the

anguish, and assist the subject to feel less helpless and dependent on his important good objects that appear to him damaged and bring out such an onerous responsibility. The end result, however, is that the contempt damages the objects even more, and may therefore lead to a vicious circle." (p. 346)

Judith Edwards (2005) says that growth (reparation) occurs through the acknowledgment of loss; Klein (1935) says that mania (manic reparation) is the inevitable outcome of denial. Now we can begin to see how an internal, psycho-social tug of war has halted progress in the African American community. Now we can understand why one step forward always seems to be accompanied by five steps back.

Herbert Rosenfeld (1959) focuses on how the individual's premonition of failure exacerbates manic reparation. Rosenfeld says, "The sense of despair relates to the individual's doubt in his capacity for reparation." Self-doubt, a lack of self-confidence, and low self-esteem are inhibiting psychological reparation in the community.

Hanna Segal (1964) agrees with this psychic tug-of-war scenario. Psychological reparation confronts and embraces the pain associated with the loss of a loved object while "manic reparation is a defense in that its aim is to repair the object in such a way that guilt and loss are never experienced" (p. 95).

Phantasy and the Unconscious

Every day we humans slip into conscious and unconscious reveries, daydreams, and even nightmares. We imagine how we'd like our future to be. We wonder if the creaking floors we hear at night mean danger. This is the common understanding of fantasy.

Klein deliberately spells "phantasy" with a *ph* to differentiate it from our normal daydreams, reveries, and fantasies. According to Klein, phantasies are created by urges and impulses arising from the body, senses, and imagination. "In the face of painful need, the infantile body together with the wishing, instinctual psyche, produces a particular phantasy" (Likierman, 2001).

According to Klein, the loved object is often destroyed in the phantasy life of the child. "Side by side with the destructive impulses in the unconscious mind both of the child and of the adult, there exists a profound urge to make sacrifices, in order to help and put right loved people who in phantasy have been harmed or destroyed" (Klein and Riviere, 1964, p. 65).

Repairing the shattered psyche is a challenge. Before health is achieved, guilt often rears its ugly head. On one hand, guilt is caused by the desire to destroy the loved object for selfish reasons. On the other, the ego seeks a way to eliminate the guilt and put the damaged loved object back together. This inner conflict recalls the story of Humpty Dumpty. In the story, Humpty decides to sit on the wall. In phantasy, the ego pushes Humpty off the wall for selfish reasons. Afterwards, the guilt-ridden ego remembers that Humpty is its friend and thus determines to repair the damage to its psyche. The ego gathers the resources of its psychic world, the king's horses and the king's men, to repair its inner representation, or phantasy, of Humpty. Understand that this violence only occurred in the psyche, *not* in external reality. Humpty never fell, nor was he pushed off the wall. It was done in the ego's phantasy world.

Klein (Klein and Riviere, 1964) says:

> "At the same time, we also play part of the good child towards his parents, which we wished to do in the past and are now acting out in the present. Thus, by reversing a situation, namely in acting towards another person as a good parent, in phantasy we re-create and enjoy the wished-for love and

goodness of our parents. But to act as good parents towards other people may also be a way of dealing with the frustrations and sufferings of the past. Our grievances against our parents for having frustrated us, together with the feelings of hate and revenge to which these have given rise in us, and again, the feelings of guilt and despair arising out of this hate and revenge because we have injured the parents whom at the same time we loved – all these, in phantasy, we may undo in retrospect (taking away some of the grounds for hatred), by playing at the same time the parts of loving parents and loving children. At the same time, in our unconscious phantasy we make good the injuries which we did in phantasy, and for which we still unconsciously feel very guilty. This *making reparation* is, in my view, a fundamental element in love and in all human relationships." (pp. 67–68)

Psychological reparation attempts to address the frustrations of the past. Intimate relationships are an excellent example. Frustrating events between husband and wife, parent and child may be the result of actual experiences in the external world or experiences from the world of phantasy. Klein (Klein and Riviere, 1964) explains:

"School life affords an opportunity for developing the experience already gained of relationship to people, and provides a field for new experiments on this line…. These new friendships, among other satisfactions, give him an opportunity for revising and improving, as it were, the early relationships with his brothers and sisters, which may have been unsatisfactory. He may actually have been aggressive towards, let us say, a brother who was weaker or younger; or it may have been mainly his unconscious sense of guilt because of hatred and jealousy which disturbed the relationship – a disturbance which may persist into grown-up life.... Some children are, as we know, incapable of making friends at school, and this is because they carry their early conflicts into a new environment. With others who can detach themselves sufficiently from their first emotional entanglements and can make friends with schoolmates, it is often found that the actual relation to brothers and sisters then improves. The new companionships prove to the child that he is able to love and is lovable, that love and goodness *exist*, and this is unconsciously felt also as a proof that he can repair harm which he has done to others in his imagination or in actual fact. Thus new friendships help in the solution of earlier emotional difficulties, without the person being aware either of the exact nature of those early troubles or of the way in which they are being solved. By all of these means the tendencies for making reparation find scope, the sense of guilt is lessened, and trust in oneself and in others is increased." (pp. 94–95)

When the phantasy pain of guilt or hatred from past experiences is decreased or diminished, individuals are then capable of establishing loving relationships (Klein and Riviere, 1964, p. 107). Psychological reparation is now doing its healing work.

The Paranoid-Schizoid and Depressive Positions

According to Klein, ego development occurs in two phases: the paranoid-schizoid position and the depressive state. Healing or destruction depends on the position that is active in the psyche. John Steiner (1992), in "The Equilibrium Between the Paranoid-Schizoid and the Depressive Positions," states, "Perhaps the most significant difference between the two positions is along the dimension of increasing integration which leads to a sense of wholeness both in the self and in object relations as the depressive position is approached."

Paranoid-schizoid position. A. A. Mason (1977) offers a clear explanation of the paranoid-schizoid position.

> "Melanie Klein divided human attitudes into two basic positions that she believed stemmed from early infancy and a certain constellation of relationships between a baby and its parents. She called one the paranoid-schizoid position, the other the depressive position. The paranoid-schizoid position is the state of mind an infant is in from birth to about three to six months, when he is dominated by paranoid-schizoid mechanisms. *Schizoid* means splitting. Infants deal with pain and frustration as though they were something bad to be split off and got rid of, like excrement. Now the consequence of taking something that is painful or bad or hurting and splitting it off

and projecting it is paranoia. The outside world will now seem filled with what has been projected into it. If a patient has a mouse phobia or a spider phobia, that is a localized form of paranoia. Paranoia is fear of a person, phobia is fear of a thing, and anxiety is fear that is diffused. They are all forms of what we call persecutory anxiety."

Steiner (1992) explains that "in the paranoid-schizoid position the chief defenses are splitting, projective identification, and idealization; the structure of the ego reflects the split into good and bad objects, and object relationships are likewise split." This position is characterized by fragmentation; imagine a mirror shattering into many pieces. Furthermore, the individual may resist integrating the many pieces, i.e., the good and bad objects.

First, the psyche decides what is good and bad. Then it takes the bad objects and projects them into other people. This is the paranoid-schizoid position, and it keeps the patient in a manic reparative state (vs. the healing reparative state). "Klein believed that the individual is threatened by sources of destructiveness from within, based on the death instinct, and that these are projected into…[an] object to create the prototype of a hostile object relationship" (Steiner, 1992). In this way, hatred exists internally before it is experienced externally in relationships.

Steiner (1992) postulated a theoretical structure to study the variety that exists within the paranoid-schizoid position. "In practice, however, we find defenses being deployed in more complex ways, and a deeper understanding of mental mechanisms has led to a distinction between different levels of organization within the paranoid-schizoid position."

Chapter 2: Psychological Reparation

Two poles exist in the paranoid-schizoid position: "normal splitting" and "pathological fragmentation." In normal splitting,

> "The immature infant has to organize his chaotic experience, and a primitive structure to the ego is provided by a split into good and bad. This reflects a measure of integration which allows a good relationship to a good object to develop by splitting off destructive impulses which are directed towards bad objects. This kind of splitting may be observed clinically, and in infant observation, as an alternation between idealized and persecutory states. If successful the ego is strengthened to the point where it can tolerate ambivalence, and the split can be lessened to usher in the depressive position. Although idealized, and hence a distortion of reality, the periods of integration, which at this stage take place in relation to good objects, can be seen as precursors of the depressive position."
> (Steiner, 1992)

Steiner states that normal splitting is healthy, and if successful, will lead to true reparation.

Pathological fragmentation is a severe type of the paranoid-schizoid position. It develops when normal splitting cannot handle extreme psychic or internal threats.

> "One such situation arises if persecutory anxiety becomes excessive, which may leave the individual feeling that his very survival is threatened. Such a threat may paradoxically

lead to further defensive fragmentation which involves minute splitting and violent projection of the fragments." (Steiner, 1992)

Steiner states that the progressive development towards wholeness is accomplished when pathological fragmentation reaches the level of normal splitting, and normal splitting "can be lessened to usher in the depressive position" (Steiner, 1992). The depressive position is the stage in the healing process we must strive toward. The depressive position is the gateway to healing and wholeness.

Depressive position. The depressive position is the challenging but courageous inner urge to acknowledge, confront, and work through the guilt and sorrow; this is the process of psychological reparation. Manic reparation (avoidance, denial) occurs when the ego attempts to avoid the depressive position (guilt, sorrow). "The infantile depressive position is the central position in the child's development. The normal development of the child and its capacity for love would seem to rest largely on how the ego works through this nodal position" (Klein, 1935).

In other words, our ability to love one another and to be unified in purpose once again depends on our working through the depressive position. If we refuse, the destructive behaviors will continue.

In Kleinian theory, "mourning is an essential process in growth of the ego and characteristically leads to what she called the depressive position in early development. The young child's arduous psychological work in this position is…central to her developmental theory" (Burch, 1989).

Hanna Segal (1964) maintained that "the depressive position marks a crucial step in the infant's development, and its working through is accompanied by a radical alteration in his view of reality" (p. 73). Only when we begin to acknowledge and work through our collective guilt and despair will healing, growth, and development take place once again (psychological reparation).

Neil Altman (2005) explored the United States' attempt at reparation following the attacks of September 11, 2001. Altman (2005) notes that what was created instead was the War on Terror, a classic example of manic reparation:

> "We view the U.S. government's response to the terrorist attacks of 2001 as a fundamentally manic response. That is, the response has been to attempt to restore a damaged sense of omnipotence and guiltlessness by constructing and attacking an enemy, Saddam Hussein, who could be easily defeated in the name of spreading North American virtues such as democracy and freedom. The fact that there was no evidence that Saddam Hussein was a threat to the United States, or that he had anything to do with the September 11 attacks, was ignored in the face of the defensive need to restore a sense of the country's omnipotence and virtue. Complications—such as the collateral damage to civil liberties in the United States, to the country's standing in the international community, and to the effort to counter real terrorist threats—were ignored in favor of the need to have a simple, black-and-white view of the world we live in, with good guys and bad guys and never the twain shall meet. In psychoanalytic terms, *there was a retreat from depressive position complexity, doubt, and sorrow* [emphasis added]." (pp. 321–322)

Restoring the Mind of Black America

Governments, communities, and individuals choose manic reparation in an effort to avoid the pain of the *depressive position*, which Klein held as the threshold of growth and development.

Segal (1964) said, "Because of these conditions, the underlying guilt which manic reparation seeks to alleviate is, in fact, not relieved, and the reparation brings no lasting satisfaction" (p. 96). Manic reparation, Segal believes, does not accept the concept of reality; it exists on the premise of magic. The individual hopes that something miraculous will cause a change.

I believe the African American community requires more psychological work than mere political action. The emptiness that existed within the community following the assassinations of our leaders created a depressive position. Replaying civil rights events in the media did not allow us to process through our tragic losses. Thus, we suffer on in the paranoid-schizoid position, avoiding the guilt and shame, projecting inner hate objects into other races, the government, each other, and ourselves. If the community continues to avoid the depressive state, progress and future growth will not occur.

In children, attention is given to the oral stage and its end, i.e., the weaning of the child from the breast. This weaning reaches its climax in the depressive position (Klein, 1935). The African American community has been weaned, cut off, from its leaders and organizations. Other events exacerbated the depressive state of the community, but these were shocks that came after the initial weaning. The purpose of the manic defense is merely to avoid the community's ego from experiencing depression. Otto Fenichel (1943) believed that the depressive position derived during weaning is the "period to which the victims of depression regress." Fenichel (1943) says,

> "The difference between a child in the 'depressive position' and the mourning adult is that the child is able to overcome its mourning by convincing itself that the real outer mother is still present while the mourning adult has really lost his object and he has to help himself through the reestablishment of 'inner good objects.'"

Once depression has been acknowledged and takes its painful place in the life of the individual or community, the desire to repair the damaged or destroyed loved objects is activated (Segal, 1964, p. 72). I believe the psychological reparation of the African American community will propel us to achieve even greater successes than were conceived during the Civil Rights Movement. Just as an infant continues to develop after being weaned from the breast, the African American community must move on and develop after the loss of its leaders and organizations. We must acknowledge, experience, and mourn this loss. With this acknowledgment will come new ideas, new creativity, and new purpose.

> "The pain of mourning experienced in the depressive position, and the reparative drives developed to restore the loved internal and external objects, are the basis of creativity and sublimation.... The...longing to recreate his lost of objects gives him the impulse to put together what has been torn asunder, to reconstruct what has been destroyed, to recreate and to create." (Segal, 1964, p. 75)

During the movement, there was much talk about "the struggle." We embraced the struggle with pride and courageously demanded equal rights in the face of violent opposition. The persistent pain of the depressive position promotes creativity; creativity enables psychological reparation—and a new, healthy perspective on life. According to Segal (1964),

> "...when the infant enters the depressive position and he is faced with feeling that he has omnipotently destroyed his mother, his guilt and despair at having lost her awaken in him the wish to restore and recreate her in order to regain her externally and internally. The same reparative wishes arise in relation to other loved objects, external and internal .... It is also the basis for creative activities, which are rooted in the infant's wish to restore and recreate his lost happiness, his lost internal objects and the harmony of his internal world. Reparative phantasies and activities resolve the anxieties of the depressive position." (p. 92)

The depressive position has the potential to lead the individual to renewal and maturity, true reparation. However, because the pain of the depressive position is often overwhelming, Steiner holds that the individual may fluctuate between paranoid-schizoid and depressive if the ego is incapable of enduring the pain. In phantasy, he may split off the good aspects of the object regardless of the condition of the actual object in reality. Steiner (1992) states, "Attempts to possess and preserve the good object are part of the depressive position and lead to a renewal of splitting, this time to prevent the loss of the good object and to protect it from attacks."

Chapter 2: Psychological Reparation

Once an individual has developed the strength to endure the integration of the good and bad, the pain of the depressive state can be endured. "The aim in this phase of the depressive position is to deny the reality of the loss of the object, and this state of mind is similar to that of the bereaved person in the early stages of mourning. In mourning, it appears as a normal stage which needs to be passed through before the subsequent experience of acknowledgement of loss can take place" (Steiner, 1992).

Steiner (1992) presents two aspects of the depressive position: "*fear* of loss of the object" and "*experience* of loss of the object" (emphasis added). Experiencing the loss will press the individual toward renewal and wholeness. When the individual experiences the loss, mourning can then take place. Steiner (1992) states that the psychic reality of the individual

> "...includes the realization of the...awareness that his love and his reparative wishes are insufficient to preserve his object which must be allowed to die, with the consequent desolation, despair, and guilt. These processes involve intense mental pain and conflict, which is part of the function of mourning to resolve."

When African Americans are in the paranoid-schizoid position, they project feelings of loss, disgrace and guilt onto one another and/or other social groups. Mason (1977) stated, "People who have an excessive paranoid-schizoid disposition will generally complain about being attacked in some way: their boss is always against them, or their wife, or their kids, or even their dog." The paranoid-schizoid position allows for little accountability or responsibility for thoughts and deeds. The blame will be placed on the projected object.

The paranoid-schizoid position resists integration of the good and painful. Rather than accepting what appears to be unbearable, the ego splits off the pain and projects it. After the assassination of our leaders, we projected our own tragic sense of loss, hopelessness, and discouragement onto ourselves and each other via crime, violence, addictions, etc.

Mason (1977) states,

> "One common mechanism occurring in the paranoid-schizoid position is projective identification. Projective identification, like other defense mechanisms, is an infantile fantasy. The mind works only in fantasy. A part of the self that is unwanted is treated like a piece of excreta, and evacuated onto an object."

Mason (1977) further states,

> "Klein believed that when the patient progressed from the paranoid position the splits came together and he entered another state of mind, called the depressive position. That, she postulated, was a normal consequence of a certain amount of integration. At first pain is dealt with in a very primitive way: it is evacuated. And objects are dealt with in a very primitive way; they are separated into good and bad. Gradually, as the capacity for tolerating an object that is not all gratifying increases, the ego takes on a more integrated view both of the object and of the self."

Chapter 2: Psychological Reparation

Manic Defenses of the African American Community

Manic defenses are mental operations the ego uses to avoid experiencing depression. In the African American community, riots are manic defenses in that they help to avoid the humiliation and despair of injustices that are experienced by the people.

Otto Fenichel (1943) believed that the depressive position experienced during weaning is the "period to which the victims of depression regress." If the birth of the African American community can be symbolically linked to the Civil Rights Movement, then our behaviors during the movement and thereafter can be understood in a new light. For example, riots in the community are a manic defense and a regression of the depressive position. "When the depressive position arises, the ego is forced (in addition to earlier defenses) to develop methods of defense which are essentially directed against 'pining' for the loved object" (Klein, 1940). Another example was when our leaders were assassinated and organizations dismantled; this weaning off of our leaders and organizations also caused us to regress, as noted by Fenichel.

The manic defense has a variety of ways it can prevent the experience of the depressive position (Klein, 1935). Substance abuse and violence in the community can be attributed to the manic defense. The community's ego has fostered a dependency on the manic defense in order to avoid overcoming the depressive position.

Furthermore, dependence on the manic defense replaces dependence on the damaged loved objects. African Americans have rendered the gains made during the Civil Rights Movement as meaningless. Instead we engage in destructive behaviors (manic defense) rather than building on the mission of our leaders and organizations.

> "In mania, however, denial is associated with
> an overactivity [*sic*], although this excess of

activity…often bears no relation to any actual results achieved. I have explained that in this state the source of the conflict is that the ego is unwilling and unable to renounce its good intern al objects and yet endeavors to escape from the perils of dependence on them as well as from its bad objects. Its attempt to detach itself from an object without at the same time completely renouncing it seems to be conditioned by an increase in the ego's own strength. It succeeds in this compromise by *denying the importance* of its good objects." (Klein, 1935)

An internal problem is currently preventing the African American community from progressing beyond the achievements of the civil rights era. Although it is possible to trace the root of the problem back to slavery, it may not be necessary to intellectually travel that distance. The respect held for the African American leaders and organizations of the Civil Rights Movement (internalized loved objects) prevents the collective ego from making the previous accomplishments appear insignificant. And while today many African American "leaders" and organizations work on civil rights-type projects, no one has been able to revive the movement itself.

"The triumph over the parents in such phantasies, through the guilt to which it gives rise, often cripples endeavors of all kinds. Some people are obliged to remain unsuccessful, because success always implies to them the humiliation or even the damage of

> somebody else, in the first place the triumph
> over parents, brothers and sister.... The effect
> is that the reparation to the loved objects,
> which in the depths of the mind are the same
> as those over which he triumphs, is again
> thwarted, and therefore guilt remains
> unrelieved.... Depression may follow, or an
> increase in manic defenses." (Klein, 1940, p.
> 134)

We appear to be the only people who do not build on past achievements. Community-based organizations tend to avoid the achievements of the civil rights heroes (loved objects). By denying what was accomplished, the community is not obliged to maintain or embrace the objectives of the heroes. The legal progress, socioeconomic opportunities, and rights obtained through the heroic efforts of the leaders are wasted. Acknowledging the blood that was shed and the physical pain that was endured to empower the community brings guilt and shame to the community. Progress through the depressive state is simply too difficult.

Denial and contempt are manic defenses that prevent the ego from undergoing the depressive position, and the African American community is definitely in a state of denial and contempt. When accepted that the loved objects cannot be repaired, the ego must refuse to accept the need for the object. "This contempt, however, is also based to some extent on denial. He must deny his impulse to make extensive and detailed reparation because he has to deny the cause for the reparation" (Klein, 1940, p. 135). Now we can begin to understand the rise in gang violence. Without such manic activity, the community would experience a depressive state over the loss of its loved objects. That pain must be avoided at all cost, even if it means engaging in gang violence. Klein (1935) says that

> "...this *disparagement of the object's importance and the contempt for it* is, I think, a specific characteristic of mania and enable the ego to effect that partial detachment which we observe side by side its hunger for objects. Such detachment which the ego cannot achieve in the depressive position."

From Steiner's (1992) perspective, healthy and true psychological reparation involves working through both the paranoid-schizoid and depressive positions. The defense mechanisms within the paranoid-schizoid position must be overcome by integrating the tolerable and intolerable realities. This will painfully lead one to the depressive state and mourning. It is within this phase that the benefit of the loss can be achieved, and true psychological reparation will occur.

Chapter 3: Social Reparations

The topic of economic reparations is of concern internationally. *The Random House Dictionary* traces the term *reparations* to the 14th century. Reparations is the making of financial amends to correct an injustice, to right a wrong. Reparations on a global scale address the economic, social, and developmental losses of nations and geopolitical regions. The term is often used in the context of war, where the loser compensates the victor a certain amount. However, in certain circumstances, the victor will compensate the losing nation. For example, the United Nations has been actively developing reparations policies for several countries that have been damaged by colonialism.

Since the 1800s, African Americans have sought social reparations (political and economic) to make amends for the tremendous losses suffered during slavery. The argument for reparations has remained essentially the same up to the present moment: during the transatlantic slave trade, we lost our culture, families, history, language, wealth, and African identity. Although the topic of social reparations only hints at psychological healing, it is important nevertheless. In this chapter we will review literature that argues for the importance of social reparations to the survival and progress of the African American community. Contributions for this section are from the following: Ronald Salzberger and Mary Turck (2004), Randall Robinson (2002), Robin D. G. Kelley (2002), Raymond Winbush (2003), William L. Banks (2001), and John Torpey (2006).

Social Reparations for African Americans: Then and Now

According to Salzberger and Turck, the idea of social reparations for African Americans was born in 1865, after the Thirteenth Amendment to the U.S. Constitution was ratified and the African slaves were freed. There were no programs in

31

place to prepare them for independence or autonomy, so Union Army General William Tecumseh Sherman issued a special order that confiscated land in the South which then became the basis for providing 40 acres of land to each of the freed Africans (Salzberger and Turck, 2004, p. 283). In 1867, member of the U.S. House of Representatives Thaddeus Stevens of Pennsylvania introduced the *Reparations Bill for the African Slaves in the United States – The First Session Fortieth Congress* (Salzberger and Turck, p. 64). The purpose of the bill was to create equality for all Americans, including African Americans. A strong supporter of reparations for African Americans,

> "Stevens spoke eloquently in support of his bill, but it never passed. His speech in support of the bill sets out…rationales for economic reparations. First, reparations are a matter of economic justice, restoring to the freed slaves some of the economic justice, restoring to the freed slaves some of the economic benefits produced by their labor and confiscated by slave-holders. Second, reparations must be made or the country will experience continuing racial hatred, inequality, and strife." (Salzberger and Turck, 2004, p. 65)

According to Winbush (2003), the long history of reparations advocacy has occurred in four stages:

> "Stage I, from 1865 to 1920, included the United States governments' attempt to compensate its newly released three million enslaved Africans from bondage. This period also saw Callie House's heroic efforts at establishing the Ex-Slave Mutual Relief,

Chapter 3: Social Reparations

Bounty and Pension Association when she organized hundreds of thousands of ex-slaves for repayment from the government. Stage II, from 1920 to 1968, saw Marcus Garvey, Queen Mother Audley Moore, and numerous Black Nationalists press for reparations by educating thousands of persons about the unpaid debt owed to Africans in America…. Stage III began in 1968 and continues today. The founding of several Black nationalist groups including the Republic of New Africa (1968), the National Coalition of Blacks for Reparations in America (1987), and James Forman's "Black Manifesto" (1969)…served as catalysts for launching what some have called the modern reparations movement… Stage IV of the movement began in 2002 with the filing of several lawsuits against corporations and ultimately the government." (pp. xii–xiii)

Today, millions of African Americans do not consider reparations as a handout; rather, it is viewed as a delayed payment. And the claim for reparations does not stop at slavery and America's unpaid financial debt. It is also concerned with the lingering impact of slavery. The claim for reparations includes all the damage that was done to the African slaves and the ongoing victimization of their descendants.

In *The Reckoning: What Blacks Owe to Each Other*, Randall Robinson (2002) discusses a comprehensive appeal for reparations. Robinson said:

"[He has] been centrally involved in the reparations movement seeking restitution to the contemporary descendents of American slaves for economic and social disadvantages

33

born of slavery and the century of government-
based racial discrimination that follow in its
train." (pp. 271–272)

Robin D. G. Kelley (2002) in *Freedom Dreams* says:

"By looking at the reparations campaign in the
United States as a social movement, we
discover that it was never entirely, or even
primarily, about money. The demand for
reparations was about social justice,
reconciliation, reconstructing the *internal* life
of Black America, and eliminating institutional
racism. This is why reparations proposals from
Black radical movements focused less on
individual payments than on securing funds
to build autonomous Black institutions,
improving community life, and in some cases
establishing a homeland that will enable
African Americans to develop a political
economy geared more toward collective needs
than toward accumulation." (p. 114)

Realizing that the damage to the African American
community consists of more than lost wages, today's Black
reparationists are seeking to heal a damaged people rather
than just fill empty pockets. Kelley (2002) further adds that
we should

"…uphold a radical concept of reparations as
more than a paycheck and an apology. It
regards the campaign as part of a many-
pronged attack on race and class oppression,
an analysis of the root cause of inequality, and
a means to mobilize African Americans to

> struggle for social change, self-transformation,
> and self-reliance." (pp. 128–129)

Although numerous books have been written about reparations, unfortunately, demands for reparations are not as vocal today as they were in the 1960s through 1990s. Most of the current literature on reparations merely reviews the attempts that were made in previous decades, including U.S. Congressman John Conyers' request in 1989 to study the validity of reparations.

Perspectives of Social Reparations

William L. Banks (2001) makes a distinction between *reparation* and *reparations*, and between African Americans as a people and as a nation. He says that "reparations (plural), is defined as compensation of remuneration required from a defeated *nation* as indemnity for damage or injury during a war" (p. 3). Given that we come from different regions or countries of Africa, we may not be a singular, distinct nation, but we are a people (p. 4).

John Torpey (2006) also distinguishes between *reparation* and *reparations*:

> "Reparation thus involves a variety of actions
> and activities that seek to restore the *status
> quo ante*. With the possible exception of
> "guarantee of non-repetition," which are
> predominantly political and legislative in
> nature, the activities that comprise reparation
> are notably legalistic in character and may or
> may not involve transfers of money. In
> contemporary usage, the notion of 'reparation'
> thus hews closer than its sibling 'reparations'
> to terms' roots in the idea of 'repair.' That is,
> reparation is more akin to the idea of

restoration of the state of affairs before the violation occurred. By contrast, reparations have come to be used almost synonymously with compensation—that is, with money transfers of a relatively direct kind. One *makes* reparation, in short, but one *pays* reparations. Paradoxically, the singular of the term connotes a multiplicity of activities, whereas the plural tends to entail only one." (p. 45)

Winbush (2003) alludes to Molefi Kete Asante's position on the benefits of reparations, which includes Asante's belief that "reparations would insure: (1) recognition of the Africans' loss, (2) compensation for the loss, (3) psychological relief for both Blacks and whites in terms of guilt and anger, and (4) national unity based on a stronger political will" (p. 10). Asante's idea of social reparations includes unification, restitution, and psychological reparation, which more closely aligns with Melanie Klein.

A somewhat skeptical John Torpey (2006), in *Making Whole What Has Been Smashed: On Reparations Politics,* explores the political ramifications of global reparations, or what he calls "reparations politics." Torpey believes that reparations politics is " a broader field encompassing such phenomena as transitional justice, apologies, and efforts at reconciliation as well" (p. 42). He is critical of those who seek amends for past injustices.

"Reparations politics begins from the assumption that *the road to the future runs through the past....* Despite frequent claims that reparations would be good for all concerned, both perpetrators and victims, reparations politics makes claims on behalf of victims and is hence unavoidably partisan....

Chapter 3: Social Reparations

The important questions concern what aims reparations seek to achieve, and whether reparations politics are well-tailored to achieve their aims." (Torpey, 2006, pp. 5–6)

Torpey (2006) says that reparations advocacy looks to correct the past instead of creating a modern vision of the future—the type of vision that fueled the many activities and achievements of the Civil Rights Movement.

> "...the spread of reparations politics is a product of particular historical circumstances—in particular, it is a response to a post-utopian context that differs sharply from the period that preceded it—and seeks to achieve some of the aims of the progressive agenda through a focus on righting the past rather than on the basis of the kind of idealized vision of the human future that drove much that went before it." (p. 7)

Torpey believes that reparations politics is a step backward in human achievement and that filing claims for past damages is counterproductive.

> "Efforts to rectify past wrongs have thus arisen in part as a substitute for expansive visions of an alternative human future of the kind that animated the socialist movements of the preceding century, which have been overwhelmingly discredited since the fall of the Berlin Wall in 1989.
> "The spread of reparations politics has thus taken place more or less simultaneously with the diffusion of multiculturalism and identity politics, on the one hand, and with a growing

concern about victims and victims' rights, on
the other…. Reparations politics has raised the
banner of the victims of oppression as groups
deserving special consideration and concern."
(Torpey, 2006, pp. 15–16)

Recognizing the comprehensive damage that has been
done to African Americans, some modern reparationists
acknowledge the need for psychological healing as well as
economic and political restitution.

"Since reparations are typically understood to
involve compensation for the effects of slavery
and its aftermath, reparations advocates almost
invariably concentrate on the economic harms
suffered by slaves and their descendents. Thus
we hear about unpaid labor, seized inheritances,
unjust enrichment, and opportunity usurped.

"In reparations circles we hear much less
often about continuing injury that is not
economic or material. There are, however,
discussions of continuing nonmaterial injuries
that we should listen to as well.

"Slavery was an insult in two senses. In
the first, slavery was a kind of moral *stain*.
Africans in America were demeaned by
slavery. Slavery also insulted in the medical
sense. *It created psychological injury*."
(Salzberger and Turck, 2004, p. 33)

Winbush says:

"…a less severe form of the violence and abuse
continued after slavery officially ended with
peonage, Black Codes, Convict Leasing,

lynchings, beatings, threats to life and property, the rise of the Klan, Jim Crow segregation, the death of Emmett Till, the race riots of the 1960s...the proliferation of white supremacist groups...the 1991 beating of Rodney King, the 1999 dragging death of James Byrd in Jasper, Texas, by four white youths, the police shooting death of Amadou Diallo in 1999, and the 2002 police beating of sixteen-year-old Donovan Jackson-Chavis, a special-education, hearing-impaired youth. All these events remind African Americans that the trauma has never really ceased and that it is likely to continue if there is no intervention." (Winbush, 2003, p. 269)

Part 2: The Civil Rights Movement

Chapter 4: Significant Revolutionaries

Long after the Civil War, the African American community tossed and turned in the belly of America until a movement was born and a new people emerged. The Civil Rights Movement gave birth to the Black community.

> "Historians consider the Civil Rights Movement to have begun in 1954. African Americans had always struggled for their rights, from the fight to free themselves from slavery in the nineteenth century to the demand for equal treatment socially, politically, and economically. However, in the years following World War II, their efforts combined into a coordinated massive appeal for justice." (Vernell, 2000, p. 12)

Freud and Klein maintained different perspectives regarding the birth of consciousness or the ego. While one held that consciousness preceded birth, the other held that it was developed after birth. I believe that the consciousness of the African American community was awakened during the Civil Rights Movement. While Marcus Garvey initiated the birth of African consciousness through his many efforts to empower those of African descent, it was during the Civil Rights Movement that the consciousness of the community was delivered, as when a mother gives birth to a child.

For the purposes of this study, we will focus on Dr. Martin Luther King, Jr., Malcolm X, and the Black Panther Party as the internalized loved objects of the community. They were the primary leaders who created the vision for the Civil Rights Movement. In fact, these men were more than leaders and organizers; they were fathers-mothers. As fathers, they stood up for us. As mothers, they nurtured and cared for the community. They gave their time, energy, and lives to rescue the community from degradation.

These men were family to us. Their pictures and posters hold honored places in our homes. We read their writings and admired them for their courage. Losing these leaders was the psychological equivalent of losing cherished members of the family.

The leaders provided the Black community with two primary functions. Dr. King promoted civil rights through nonviolent direct action. Malcolm X promoted civil rights "by any means necessary" including, to quote the title of one of his speeches, "The Ballot or the Bullet." The Black Panther Party continued the efforts of Malcolm X through an organizational implementation of Malcolm's philosophy of self-preservation.

The leaders of the movement provided the African American community with a new perspective of Black men. The leaders portrayed a strong ideal of the Black man in America. The leaders showed women what should be expected from the Black man.

The community had faith in the leaders to speak on behalf of their well-being. Their mere presence provided the community with a sense of safety. They gave Black men confidence to be men and Black women comfort in having strong Black men around. The leaders equipped the community with the ability to function through the mire of a dysfunctional country.

From Frederick Douglass to Marcus Garvey, many worthy African American leaders and organizations made significant contributions during the Civil Rights Movement, but in this study I will focus on those whom I feel made the greatest impact: Dr. King, Malcolm X, and the Black Panther Party.

Dr. King, Malcolm X, and the Black Panther Party raised awareness of our inherent goodness as a people. Their messages and methods enhanced the community's sense of self and identity. Dr. King has been identified as a king, and Malcolm X as a prince. The Black Panther Party brought power to the people.

I selected these leaders based on their impact on the community and the effect of their removal from the community. Erich Fromm (1969) has stated that "the most beautiful as well as the most ugly inclinations of man are not part of a fixed and biologically given human nature, but result from the social process which creates man" (pp. 10–11).

Contributions for the chapters in Part 3 are from the following: Erich Fromm (1969), Marjorie Vernell (2000), Stephen B. Oates (1994), Marshall Frady (2002), Stephan Thernstrom and Abigail Thernstrom (2000), Robert E. Terrill (2004), Joe Wood (1992), John Henrik Clarke (1969/1993), William W. Sales, Jr. (1994), Cornel West (1993), Sudhi Rajiv (1992), Joan Didion (2003), Reginald Major (1971), William Lee Brent (1996), Sol Stern (2003), David Hilliard (2006), Nora Sayre (2003), Cle "Bone" Sloan (2005), Alex Haley and Malcolm X (1965), Dennis Combs, et al. (2006), Wilford R. Bion (1961), Melanie Klein (1940), Na'im Akbar (1991), Amos N. Wilson (1991), Joost A. M. Meerloo (1956), Earl Ofari Hutchinson (1990), Paul Schimmel (1998), Joseph Sandler (1995 and 2003), Lottie L. Joiner (2008), and Karen Horney (1945).

Chapter 5: Martin Luther King, Jr.

The African American community was born on December 5, 1955, at a rally in Montgomery, Alabama. This rally was held in response to the inhumane treatment of African Americans. The leader of this event was Dr. Martin Luther King, Jr. He became a loved object who was internalized by the community. Stephen B. Oates (1994) recorded Dr. King's "delivery." Dr. King said,

> "When the history books are written in the future, somebody will have to say, 'There lived a race of people, of Black people, of people who had the moral courage to stand up for their rights. And thereby they injected a new meaning into the veins of history and civilization.'" (p. 71)

After Dr. King concluded his speech, Oates says, "He sat down, trembling from his effort. Across the church, people were yelling and waving their arms, clapping and singing as he had never seen them do before" (p. 72). This event marked a new beginning and gave life to a people. The African American community was nurtured by the leadership or parenting of Dr. King. Oates (1994) adds:

> "Yet there was 'a divine dimension' at work here, too. As the Almighty labored to create 'a harmony out of the discords of the universe,' King mused, he had selected Montgomery, Alabama, 'as the proving ground for the struggle and triumph of freedom and justice in America.' And was this not symbolically significant? For Montgomery was the

birthplace and first capital of the old slave-
based Confederacy. How sublime it would be to
transform this 'cradle of the Confederacy' into
a cradle of freedom and brotherhood." (p. 73)

Perhaps Montgomery should be considered the cradle of
the African American community within the South! The
community, at that moment, was born anew. Everyone was
accepted in the African American family, and nothing
separated them. There was no house Negro or field Negro.
This movement brought about a new birth and a new life. It
also may be said that although there were African Americans,
there was no community until the Civil Rights Movement
began.

As a parental figure and loved object,

"King imparted his philosophy at twice-
weekly mass meetings, Black Montgomery's
unique contribution to American Negro
protest. King himself stressed the significance
of the mass meetings: they cut across class
lines, he said, and brought 'the Ph.D.'s, the
M.D.'s, and the No D's' together in a common
cause, binding the Negro community together
as no other civil-rights action had ever done."
(Oates, 1994, p. 78)

Oates says that the judge who convicted King for leading
the nonviolent protest

"...had convicted every Negro in Montgomery.
For they were all bound together in a common
purpose, drawn close by their shared trials and
by the tactics of their opponents. Their
opponents could not understand what was

46

going on in Montgomery because their methods were aimed at the old Negro. But they were dealing with a new Negro in the South today, a Negro 'with a new sense of dignity and destiny.'" (p. 97)

King's impact was not restricted solely to the South. Although his message put the spotlight on the sick, segregated South, he became the leader, parent, and loved object of the African American community nationwide.

Marshall Frady (2002) also felt that King's first speech in Montgomery marked the birth of the African American community. The community's response inspired him to write that "it had become, in fact, the birth of all the mass meetings" (p. 34).

King was not without his faults. Perhaps the community's paranoid-schizoid mechanism let them see a good King and a bad King (Klein would refer to this as good breast and bad breast). Or the community may have reached a point where King was accepted as a whole object rather than a partial object.

> "The fact is, King was always to fail more often than he would succeed. But throughout his confoundments since Montgomery, including now Albany, he yet remarkably seemed to keep growing—as if only magnified by his defeats—as, to the great masses of Black Americans in those barren segregationist times, still the single most auspicious and moving figure of protest and hope, whether availing or not." (Frady, 2002, pp. 96–97)

King's role as father-leader was solidified throughout the community. "Under King's leadership, what started as a one-day gesture of protest against the mistreatment of Black people on local buses became a major long-term commitment, supported by almost the entire Black community" (Thernstrom and Thernstrom, 2000, pp. 120–121).

The internalization of King as a loved object transformed the terrorized community into a hopeful one. Even in the midst of danger, the community felt that they had all the hope and security they needed to face the world.

Chapter 6: Malcolm X

Whereas King's labor pangs occurred in the South, Malcolm X brought consciousness to the community in the North. It is probably best to consider their role as loved objects separately rather than comparatively. What Malcolm X meant to the community is not the same as what Martin meant. Their methods were different, but their goals were the same. "Malcolm's audience most often is understood to consist of African Americans in search of a viable identity" (Terrill, 2004, p. 8). Malcolm's presence offered pride and identity, and today he holds a significant role in the internal world of the community.

Joe Wood (1992) understands the importance of internalizing Malcolm within the African American psyche. He believes that Malcolm is an icon that must be embraced and internalized. He is an internalized loved object, the parent of our internal reality. Wood says that "a people needs to feel a spirit and to possess its own icons: African America and all Black people need Malcolm" (p. 16).

Clarke describes how Malcolm X developed the community's self-esteem and identity. "Malcolm X preached Black pride, Black redemption, Black reaffirmation, and he gave the Black woman the image of a Black man that she could respect" (Clarke, 1969/1993, p. 40). The significance of his presence and providence cannot be denied. As the loved object of the community, Malcolm X established an inner presence of strength and Black righteousness.

In *From Civil Rights to Black Liberation*, William W. Sales, Jr. (1994) describes Malcolm X's influence within the community. He describes his leadership as pragmatic and focused on the deplorable conditions of inner city Blacks.

"People believed and followed Malcolm X not out of an emotional attachment to his charisma. The basis of his leadership was that he gave back to his followers, in a more highly refined and clarified form, ideas and insights which in fact were rooted in their experiences…. In fact, Malcolm's charisma and leadership were based on a very low-keyed method of personal contact and one-on-one encounters with the Black masses." (p. 57)

Malcolm X was not some distant celebrity icon. He was of the people and for the people. People related to him as if they knew him personally. He was concerned about their cares and fears, just like a parent would be. Malcolm X was not a symbol of the masses; he was a symbol of the righteous, good, Black self.

While Sales (1994) portrays both Malcolm X and Dr. King as present within the internal world of African American youth, he believes that "among African American youth today, the image of Malcolm X rivals and perhaps outshines that of Dr. Martin Luther King, Jr. as a Black icon and [in his] commitment to Black people" (p. 212). These youth are not contemporaries of the Civil Rights Movement; they are children of the movement.

During Black History Month we take the time to remember the role and impact of Malcolm X. This remembering helps to confront the loss; meanwhile, during the other 11 months of the year, the community avoids the realization of the empty space created by his death.

Although many have attributed the development of African American pride and awareness to Malcolm X, some view his efforts as empty, vague, and missing the mark. Within the African American community there is a constant great divide: NAACP vs. UNIA-Marcus Garvey; W.E.B. DuBois vs. Booker T. Washington; and Dr. King vs. Malcolm X. African

Chapter 6: Malcolm X

Americans may not unanimously adhere to the loved object status of Malcolm X, just as some did not embrace Dr. King. For example, Cornel West (1993), author of *Race Matters,* considers Malcolm X an ambiguous leader within the African American community and Civil Rights Movement.

"In Malcolm the Blacks had a leader who symbolized their suffering and voiced their aspirations. He knew the thinking and language of the ghetto...he would recreate for his audience visibly the indignities they were subjected to" (Rajiv, 1992, p. 96). Malcolm's leadership and direct personal connection with the community forged a powerful relationship. "Power was the subject of many speeches that Malcolm made.... This power was derived from a sense of integrity so that the Blacks could get organized and fight from a position of strength. In the process Malcolm X, became the moral, mental and spiritual reformer of the Black Americans" (Rajiv, p. 103).

The loss of Malcolm X in 1965 was an extremely traumatic event within the African American community. It was devastating. When he died, a part of us died with him, including his fearlessness, dedication, energy, and moral vision. His eulogy, given by the late actor Ossie Davis, put into words the impact of his death. In *The Autobiography of Malcolm X* (Haley and Malcolm X, 1965), an excerpt of Davis' speech vividly illustrates an awareness of the lost object:

> "Here—at this final hour, in this quiet place, Harlem has come to bid farewell to one of its brightest hopes—extinguished now, and gone from us forever.... Malcolm was our manhood, our living, Black manhood! This was his meaning to his people. And, in honoring him, we honor the best in ourselves.... And we will know him then for what he was and is—a Prince—our own Black shining Prince!—who didn't hesitate to die, because he loved us so." (p. 521)

Restoring the Mind of Black America

Malcolm X provided the African American community with unity and positive self-consciousness, an awareness of and appreciation for the Black self. His leadership initiated progressiveness within the community. However, the community has not been able to repair the loss of Malcolm's leadership, and what he initiated died with him.

Chapter 7: The Black Panther Party

In October 1966, Huey P. Newton and Bobby Seale founded the Black Panther Party in Oakland, California. "From the beginning, they defined themselves as a revolutionary political group" (Didion, 2003, p. 676). The "Black Panther" name was taken from the badge of the Freedom Party in Lowndes County, Alabama (p. 676). The Black Panthers gave the African American community practical, day-to-day guidance on how to deal with police harassment, poverty, racism, discrimination, and injustice.

"The Panthers were a logical development of earlier Black revolutionary programs, particularly those of...the Muslims, Malcolm X, and the more activist civil rights organizations such as SNCC" (Major, 1971, p. 63). Panther leader Eldridge Cleaver "decided that the Panthers were in fact carrying on Malcolm's program and became the Minister of Information" (p. 66). Cleaver and other African Americans internalized Malcolm X as a loved object while simultaneously maintaining the psychological reparation that was being facilitated by the Black Panther Party (Major, 1971). "All claimed loyalty to Malcolm's memory, and each felt that Black people were the only ones qualified to determine the future and character of the Black community" (p. 67).

The Black Panther Party embraced each member of the African American community with a parental acceptance and concern and as a result, became a loved object within the community.

> "When Eldridge [Cleaver] raised his fist in the air and shouted with pride that the street niggers [*sic*] had finally gotten their shit together, he was talking about what Marx had called the lumpenproletariat—the brothers and sisters off the block, the pimps, hustlers,

thieves, and robbers—as the principle targets of the Panthers' organizing efforts. This abused, rejected, seemingly worthless mass would soon become the backbone of the Black Panther Party, the foot soldiers who would challenge the black bourgeoisie's hold over black communities throughout the nation. They would constitute both the Party's strength and its greatest weakness, because, as the saying goes, you can't make a house nigger out of a street nigger overnight." (Brent, 1996, p. 91)

The Panthers' unconditional acceptance of everyone in the community provided the party with a constituency and a ready-made family.

Sol Stern (2003) does not consider the Black Panther Party to be a dominant force within the Black community. He describes their role as slightly better than futile. "By any yardstick used by the civil-rights movement, the Panther organization is not yet very important or effective. The Panthers' political influence in the Negro community remains marginal" (p. 624). Stern is at odds with the majority of civil rights scholars.

Power to the People!

The Panthers developed a Ten Point Platform and Program to express their grievances about African American poverty and political disenfranchisement. All members had to memorize and follow the ten points. The purpose of the platform was to both promote the tenets of the Black Panther Party and to give the community a powerful vision of justice and equality. This manifesto appealed to African Americans because it addressed urgent issues such as poverty, housing, education, police brutality, and more.

THE BLACK PANTHER PARTY
Ten Point Platform & Program
WHAT WE WANT, WHAT WE BELIEVE

1. WE WANT freedom. We want power to determine the destiny of our Black Community. WE BELIEVE that Black people will not be free until we are able to determine our destiny.

2. WE WANT full employment for our people. WE BELIEVE that the federal government is responsible and obligated to give every man employment or a guaranteed income. We believe that if the white American businessmen will not give full employment, then the means of production should be taken from the businessmen and placed in the community so that the people of the community can organize and employ all of its people and give a high standard of living.

3. WE WANT an end to the robbery by the CAPITALISTS of our Black Community. WE BELIEVE that this racist government has robbed us and now we are demanding the overdue debt of forty acres and two mules. Forty acres and two mules were promised 100 years ago as restitution for slave labor and mass murder of Black people. We will accept the payment in currency, which will be distributed, to our many communities. The Germans are now aiding the Jews in Israel for the genocide of the Jewish people. The Germans murdered six million Jews. The American racist has taken part in the slaughter of over fifty million Black people; therefore, we feel that this is a modest demand that we make.

4. WE WANT decent housing, fit for the shelter of human beings. WE BELIEVE that if the white landlords will not give decent housing to our Black community, then the housing and the land should be made into cooperatives so that our community, with government aid, can build and make decent housing for its people.

5. WE WANT education for our people that exposes the true nature of this decadent American society. We want education that teaches us our true history and our role in the present-day society. WE BELIEVE in an educational system that will give to our people knowledge of self. If a man does not have knowledge of himself and his position in society and the world, then he has little chance to relate to anything else.

6. WE WANT all Black men to be exempt from military service. WE BELIEVE that Black people should not be forced to fight in the military service to defend a racist government that does not protect us. We will not fight and kill other people of color in the world who, like Black people, are being victimized by the white racist government of America. We will protect ourselves from the force and violence of the racist police and the racist military, by whatever means necessary.

7. WE WANT an immediate end to POLICE BRUTALITY and MURDER of Black people. WE BELIEVE we can end police brutality in our Black community by organizing Black self-defense groups from racist police oppression and brutality. The Second Amendment to the Constitution of the United States gives a right to bear arms. We therefore believe that all Black people should arm themselves for self-defense.

8. WE WANT freedom for all Black men held in federal, state, county and city prisons and jails. WE BELIEVE that all Black people should be released from the many jails and prisons because they have not received a fair and impartial trial.

9. WE WANT all Black people when brought to trail to be tried in court by a jury of their peer group or people from their Black communities, as defined by the Constitution of the United States. WE BELIEVE that the courts should follow the United States Constitution so that Black people

will receive fair trials. The 14th Amendment of the U.S. Constitution gives a man a right to be tried by his peer group. A peer is a person from a similar economic, social, religious, geographical, environmental, historical and racial background. To do this the court will be forced to select a jury from the Black community from which the Black defendant came. We have been, and are being tried by all-white juries that have no understanding of the "average reasoning man" of the Black community.

10. WE WANT land, bread, housing, education, clothing, justice and peace. And as our major political objective, a United Nations-supervised plebiscite to be held throughout the Black colony in which only Black colonial subjects will be allowed to participate, for the purpose of determining the will of Black people as to their national destiny. (Hilliard, 2006, pp. 31–34)

The Ten Point Platform expressed the hopes and dreams of African Americans. As the Panthers fearlessly promoted the heartfelt desires of the community, the organization became an internalized loved object. Each of the Ten Points demonstrates the party's concern for the community. The organization stood as a citadel against the morbid onslaught of institutionalized, government-sanctioned hatred, racism, and police brutality. The Panthers became the vanguard for many during the civil rights era.

Founder Huey P. Newton educated African Americans about their constitutional rights. He specifically wanted to end police brutality (Hilliard, 2006).

> "Huey never left home without his law book. Much has been said about the Black Panthers and guns; however, Huey's fixation with the law is rarely mentioned. Whenever he came across a policeman harassing a Black citizen,

he would stand off to the side and recite
relevant passages and penal codes within
earshot of the cop. Members of the Black
community were shocked. Never had Black
men, much less *armed* Black men, stood up to
the police for the people. As a result, two things
happened: many brothers came right out of jail
and joined the party; but more importantly,
murder and police brutality statistics fell
sharply." (p. 38)

The Black Panther Party defended the community from
attack. The Panthers created a refuge of knowledge and
awareness that helped shield the community from the brutal
effects of hatred, racism, and injustice. The party empowered
the community with knowledge. Nora Sayre (2003) said,
"They may be the only group in the country which reaches
both educated and uneducated people" (p. 855).

Unlike the demise of Malcolm X and Martin Luther King,
Jr. by assassination, the Black Panther Party was dismantled
by the United States government. David Hilliard (2006), a
member of the Black Panther Party, stated, "Many of our
members were targeted, hunted down, and imprisoned" (p. 142).

The Panthers were consistently targeted for annihilation.

"By February 2, 1971, FBI central command
solicited no less than twenty-nine field offices
to submit even more proposals and ideas on
how to best disrupt local BPP chapters,
especially the party's national headquarters in
Oakland. The bureau command believed its
four-year-long war against Huey P. Newton
and the Black Panther Party was nearing
victory." (p. 147)

The destruction of the Black Panther Party brought an
end to the Civil Rights Movement. The awakening of the

Chapter 7: The Black Panther Party

African American community and the birth of a people's identity, purpose, and passion abruptly ended with the loss of the loved objects. The community has never truly mourned the Black Panthers, and as a result, we have never truly recovered from the loss.

Chapter 8: Post-Civil Rights and Manic Reparation

The loss of the leaders caused havoc within the community. Their absence created a great void. This loss created an urgency to alleviate the pain rather than process through it, which led to manic reparation. Paul Schimmel (1998) states that

> "Manic reparation manifests as a compulsive need to put things right, and a propensity to react, rather than to reflect and respond. Such reactive doing serves to avoid realities: both the real complexities and difficulties of a situation, and the feelings of doubt and uncertainty, the 'depressive anxieties', engendered by it."

Manic reparation encourages the community to "move on" and "get over it" rather than reflecting on the loss and embracing the pain.

As discussed earlier, the unconscious seeks to repair and integrate the damaged parts of the soul while enduring the Kleinian depressive position. Remember, the function of psychological reparation is to process through our most difficult, disturbing emotions. When our leaders were assassinated and our organizations were disempowered, our souls cried out for an end to violence and racism. Psychological reparation might have done its good work had it not been undermined by the disruptive forces of the government, including the FBI and COINTELPRO. Psychological reparation became misguided, misdirected, and mishandled. The community fell apart and became manic at every turn with gang violence, substance abuse, and diminished self-esteem.

Restoring the Mind of Black America

This gave rise to the unconscious belief that reparation was impossible, the damage to the community, irreparable. The "anguish of wanting to repair so totally damaged an object stems from the fact that this is experienced as a vastly demanding task" (Hinshelwood, 1991, p. 346). Our sense of hopelessness has made us very contemptuous of self and one another. "The end result…is that the contempt damages the objects even more, and may therefore lead to a vicious circle" (Hinshelwood, 1991, p. 346). Simply, it hurts too much to deal with what happened to our leaders, organizations, and movement as a whole. This is not just a community-wide issue. Individually, we each have been infected with guilt, hopelessness, and rage.

During the Civil Rights Movement, with the internalization of the loved objects (leaders and organizations), the African American community began to grow and develop. The leaders and organizations symbolically held the community in their arms and stood up against the ravenous wolves that threatened to devour the people.

After the death of our organizations and leaders, African Americans became apathetic. The community turned to violence instead of vigor, silence instead of strength, and enemies instead of an entourage. We took a wrong turn into the paranoid-schizoid position.

Klein's theory of object relations helps us understand the impact of the destruction of the loved objects on the psyche of the African American community. Because the movement's leaders and organizations had been internalized within the phantasies of the African American community, their demise had a severe impact upon the community.

Although Freud is not considered an object relations theorist, he did provide a pivotal starting point for the paradigm. Freud's (1917) paper, "Mourning and Melancholia," has been acknowledged as the origin of internal objects. Freud uses the term *object* and considers the impact of losing an internalized object. Although Freud does not precisely describe internalization, the idea is present. Speaking of melancholia, Freud (1917) says,

> "In one set of cases it is evident that melancholia too maybe the reaction to the loss of a loved object…. In yet other cases one feels justified in maintaining the belief that a loss of this kind has occurred, but one cannot see clearly what it is that has been lost, and it is all the more reasonable to suppose that the patient cannot consciously perceive what he has lost either. This, indeed, might be so even if the patient is aware of the loss which has given rise to his melancholia, but only in the sense that he knows *whom* he has lost but not *what* he has lost in him."

Although Freud was not speaking expressly on the subject of internalization of the object, he was speaking to the subject. As for the African American community and the loss of its leaders, the community also knew who was lost, but not what was lost *in* them.

This great loss is consistent with Freud's (1917) statement that "one cannot see clearly what it is that has been lost, and…the patient cannot consciously perceive what he has lost either." When the civil rights leaders were killed, it was not clear how devastating the loss would be for the community. Freud (1917) points out that

> "The distinguishing mental features of melancholia are a profoundly painful dejection, cessation of interest in the outside world, loss of the capacity to love, inhibition of all activity, and a lowering of the self-

regarding feelings to a degree that finds
utterance in self-reproaches and self-reviling,
and culminates in a delusional expectation of
punishment."

Where pride, brotherly love, and unity once reigned in
the community—because these attributes were embodied
within our internalized loved objects (leaders and
organizations)—today the loss of the loved objects has created
a loss of self. As a result, crime, self-hate, and apathy are all
present within the African American community.

Joseph Sandler, M.D. (2003) relates the internalization
of the loved object to maintaining a sense of safety. Without
question, the African American community has lived under
the constant threat of death and suffering. During the civil
rights era, lynch mobs, the KKK, and some police officers
deprived the African American community of a sense of safety
and security. However, the African American leaders and
organizations protected the community with their fearless
advocacy. Sandler (2003) says,

"The feeling of safety is so much a part of us
that we take it for granted. It is more than a
simple absence of discomfort or anxiety, but a
very definite feeling quality, and we can regard
much of ordinary everyday behavior as a
means of maintaining a minimum level of
safety feeling. Much normal behavior as well
as many clinical phenomena (such as certain
types of psychotic behavior and the addictions)
can be more fully understood in terms of the
ego's attempt to preserve this level of safety."
(p. 14)

Chapter 8: Post-Civil Rights and Manic Reparation

Sandler later adds, "From a psychoanalytic point of view we can assume that the child's reaction to separation, the accompanying anxiety and the means that child adopts to try to regain some feeling of safety, become internalized in an internal object relationship" (p. 15). We are driven by the unconscious need to feel safe. "In short, in these unconscious processes, subjective mental representations are acted upon in order to master constant threats to the integrity of the self and therefore to the individual's feelings of safety and security" (Sandler, 2003, p. 24). The loss of our leaders and organizations created an internal void. Without their protective covering, fear and danger have been a constant presence in our lives.

Psychological reparation requires determination to work through fear, guilt, and sorrow. It appears the community refuses to embark on this healing journey, opting instead for a "What's the use?" attitude. We appear to have settled into a state of utter hopelessness. Instead of building the community, many prefer to move to a different one. The struggle has ebbed. Our fight for human rights and respect as a people has devolved into individual empowerment. Without group empowerment, however, there can be no respect for the individual.

"While the sources of hopelessness are always unconscious, the feeling itself can be fairly conscious. A person may have a pervasive sense of doom. Or he may take a resigned attitude toward life in general, expecting nothing good, feeling simply that life must be endured. Or he may express it in philosophical terms, saying in effect that life is essentially tragic and only fools deceive themselves about man's unalterable fate." (Horney, 1945, p. 182)

Clearly the community is in a state of manic reparation. Rather than continuing the fight for civil rights and experiencing the pain of the loss of the internalized loved objects, we engage in only a few efforts that will help restore health and sanity. Mostly we are distracted by entertainment, sports, and trying to survive the criminal element in our neighborhoods. In our state of manic reparation, we view the work of our leaders with constant scrutiny, suspicion, and criticism.

Clearly the community's external reality exacerbates our internal pain. Lottie L. Joiner (2008) interviewed Terrie Williams, a publicist for Hollywood celebrities, in the NAACP's *The Crisis* magazine. Williams believes her personal pain exemplifies the ubiquitous suffering of the African American community.

> "Many of us, we are either undiagnosed or underdiagnosed. I think that all of us inherit the pain of our parents, no matter how loving and well-intentioned they are…. So if you don't ever talk about the things that happened to you, it sits inside you and it festers. We self-medicate through drugs, through alcohol, with food, with gambling, with shopping when we don't have a dime; anything to ease the pain." (p. 26)

In the documentary *Bastards of the Party* (2005), Cle "Bone" Sloan examines the unconscious response of the community to the loss of civil rights leaders and organizations. Sloan stated that "from 1969, 71, 72 we started blowing each other's brains out. Sixty-five, we were calling each other 'brothers.' That's just a five year span. I'm saying how did we go from being brothers in five years, to kill that nigger?" The answer is we neglected the true reparation of civil rights to manic reparation thereafter. The removal of Malcolm X and Dr. King created a nightmare abyss within the soul of the community.

> "But in the political arena Black self-assertion was destroyed by assassination.... Thus the rulers of America kept the Negroes in subjugation by consciously and systematically emasculating their leadership. The leaders who refused to become the tools of the white power structure were ostracized or jailed.... By crushing Black leaders and inflating the images of Uncle Toms from a political world of sport and play, the mass media were able to channel and control the aspirations and goals of the Black masses." (Rajiv, 1992, p. 130)

The assassination of King and Malcolm X and the dismantling of the Panthers created widespread paranoia within the community. In "Perceived Racism as a Predictor of Paranoia among African Americans," Combs, et al. (2006) found that paranoia blocks the ability of the community to work collectively toward psychological reparation. For example, the fear of racism does not require it to be evident; the perception of racism is as powerful as racism itself. "Thus, it is possible that perceived racism would be related to cultural mistrust and nonclinical paranoia due to their foundation in real-world experiences and perceptions" (p. 89).

Perhaps the most significant sign of the pervasive hopelessness that plagues the community is the lack of unity. It is very difficult to struggle alone against racism and injustice. There is power in numbers. Yet our paranoia is focused on one another. Since we do not trust our brothers and sisters, our neighbors, our own people, we cannot achieve unity.

Restoring the Mind of Black America

Experiences in Groups (Bion, 1961) details the dynamics that are present within a group or community. This work shows how assembling together does not necessarily mean that the group is unified in purpose. The problems we face must be recognized by all as problems that affect the entire community. The genius of the civil rights leaders was their ability to forge unity among a suspicious, seemingly disparate people. Through the power of their words and their courageous actions, they persuaded the community to work together for the benefit of all. "In the treatment of a group it must be displayed as a problem of the group" (p. 11).

The failure of the community to come together as a unified group illustrates the profound depth of our grief. Melanie Klein (1940) writes, "The object which is being mourned is the mother's breast and all that the breast and the milk have come to stand for in the infant's mind: namely, love, goodness and security" (p. 126). This is what we lost at the close of the Civil Rights Movement: love, goodness, and security as displayed by our leaders and organizations (the good breast). Furthermore, Klein says, "As a result of the failure of the act of reparation, the ego has to resort again and again to obsession and manic defenses" (p. 133). We are trapped in a vicious cycle.

In *Visions for Black Men,* Na'im Akbar (1991) identifies the natural developmental process from malehood to manhood. Malehood is a state of greed and selfishness; manhood embraces accountability and responsibility. Malehood emerges from manic reparation; manhood, from reparation (healing). The African American community has maintained a state of malehood since the abrupt ending of the Civil Rights Movement. According to Akbar, the community is stuck in a state of arrested development. No reparation can take place as long as the community stays trapped in maladaptive Black malehood. Gang violence and crime are daily examples of Black malehood that is trapped in the manic state. Black malehood paranoia prevents the community from advocating for human rights as a unified body.

"But all of us are suffering from the same disease. It's called 'plantation psychosis' and we have a serious mental disorder. We are working toward our own destruction without realizing it. It is important to understand that when African people are in opposition to themselves they are mentally ill. That's what mental illness is. When you work against your own survival, you are 'crazy.' " (Akbar, 1991, p. 31)

In *Understanding Black Adolescent Male Violence*, Amos Wilson (1991) observes the violent effects of manic reparation in the community. Wilson calls this type of manic reparation "displaced aggression," and it has led to

"...horizontal or Black-on-Black violence; various forms of self-depreciation, depreciation of other Blacks, self-defeat, self-narcotization, self-destruction, disruption and/ or destruction of the social and physical environment and wide-spread social rebelliousness, particularly among the youth." (p.12)

In *The Rape of the Mind*, Joost A. M. Meerloo (1956) describes how mental health is sabotaged through brainwashing and thought control (also known as "menticide"). These fear tactics keep the individual in a perpetual survival mentality. Meerloo meticulously explains why, and to some extent how, people are induced to side with and identify with the enemy, the brainwasher. This is also known as Stockholm syndrome, in which kidnap victims (slaves) develop an emotional dependence and attachment to their captors. Brainwashing and thought control cripple critical thinking abilities. Indeed, brainwashing has led to our trust of outsiders and mistrust of each other. Because the community has been brainwashed on many different levels, we have not understood the power of unity, nor have we been able to internally repair negative defense mechanisms by properly mourning the lost loved objects (leaders and organizations).

In *The Mugging of Black America*, Earl Ofari Hutchinson (1990) reveals manipulative schemes that have undermined African American unity and promoted violence within the community. For example, criminal activity has become accepted in the community and even leveraged by "leaders," and this has led to an increase in arrests, raids, and surveillance cameras in our neighborhoods. These activities further exacerbate paranoia and manic states within the community. Attempts at reparation, to become self-sufficient and healthy, to take pride in self and the community, are undermined.

Many know about the Watts riots, but few know of the efforts made within Watts toward reparation. The Sons of Watts, an employment training program, was determined to change the manic state of the community. However,

> "...the Sons soon ran into problems. The police and public officials, plainly uncomfortable with the thought of Blacks running community programs, threw up obstacles. They refused to grant building and use permits, turned down funding requests and harassed members. Frustrated, and angry over the interference, many of the Sons soon began to drift away. One by one the businesses closed and the patrol disbanded. By 1970, the Sons of Watts had ceased to exist." (Hutchinson, 1990, p. 69)

Chapter 8: Post-Civil Rights and Manic Reparation

As Hutchinson states, many leaders and organizations have attempted psychological and social reparation over the years, but the community has been blocked at every turn. Moreover, the media's unceasing campaign to blame the victims of racism, discrimination, and injustice has deepened the community's manic defenses.

Given the current state of the African American community, the question remains: Is true reparation even possible?

Part 3: Community Activists Speak

Chapter 9: Reparation in the Trenches

"Many suggestions and documents written;
many directions for the end that was given;
they gave us pieces of silver and pieces of gold.
Tell me, who'll pay reparations on my soul?"
— Gil Scott-Heron (1970)

The participants in this study are actively involved within their community. Some are educators, juvenile probation officers, community mentors, political advocates, and community activists. They were selected for their active involvement within the community. These participants vary in age and experience; however, they all acknowledge the void that exists within the African American community as a result of the loss of the civil rights leaders and the Black Panther Party. Their ages range from 28 to 70. Their experience ranges from knowledge through books and documentaries to marching with Dr. King.

Because of their uncanny ability to honestly acknowledge how the absence of the leaders has caused the African American community to digress, I found these participants to be very valid for the purposes of this study.

While acknowledging the new breed of post-civil rights Black leaders, they consider most to be shallow and driven by motives antithetical to the community. However, the participants themselves are accepted by many as legitimate leaders. Schimmel (1998) says that "manic reparation is more than the expression of a wish to cure; it is driven by a *need* to cure" (emphasis added). The participants I selected for this study are driven by a need to cure the condition of their brothers and sisters in the community. They offer a style of leadership that harkens back to Dr. King, Malcolm X, and other civil rights leaders. They are involved, even at their own expense. They seek to lead by example, not just empty rhetoric. Their lives are devoted to service.

As you will see, the participants clearly expressed sorrow and despair at the loss of the civil rights leaders and the Black Panther Party. Manic defenses of anger, confusion, disappointment, and frustration are clearly described in each portrait.

Chapter 10: Solomon

Solomon believes that White America did not want Black America to hear the message of Malcolm X. Dr. King was a more tolerable leader for Blacks.

Solomon learned about Malcolm X from his brother. He says that his brother "chose Malcolm X, and I know that I would have chosen Malcolm X because as a teenager, nonviolent protest just would not've appealed."

Although Solomon was only a child during the Civil Rights Movement, his later study of Malcolm made him significant in Solomon's life. Once, he watched a television documentary about Malcolm, and that had a profound effect on his psyche. "I just thought that was a deep brother that really cared. Really, really understood what was going on. I was very impressed." At this point in my interview of him, Solomon seemed lost in his thoughts for a moment. Clearly he saw Malcolm as a father figure, a provider of wisdom who "really cared" about the people.

Malcolm X made it clear to anyone who would listen that African Americans had been wronged. Solomon stated:

> "If there was something you didn't realize, or if a part of your brain had been washed to accept injustices, when he exposed them, you realized that, yeah, I was wronged here, too. Here is another place I was wronged. He exposed a lot of that to a lot of people."

Malcolm X was such a paragon of Black manhood that Solomon says his brother chose Malcolm over his father.

> "Some things that my brother shared with me was that my dad was afraid and didn't want

him to follow Malcolm X. And so it started his rebellion from the family because he couldn't see it any other way. So it brought a division between him and my dad that never really healed. It just never mended because he felt so strongly about what Malcolm X and consequently the Black Panther Party was doing. My dad probably feared for his son's life. He didn't want him involved."

Many African Americans shared the feelings of Solomon's brother. They embraced Malcolm as their leader, protector, and father figure. The fatherless had a father in Malcolm X.

Solomon credits Malcolm X with awakening the community out of the sleep of ignorance. While the remnant of slavery darkened the minds of the Black community, Solomon states that Malcolm

"...enlightened us. He talked about the chains, the shackles that was taken off our ankles and placed on our brains. That's when it—well, I shouldn't say that's when it happened, but that's my memory of seeing it happen. We got shackled up real bad on the brain, and a lot of us never got those shackles off.... Malcolm X was the key to unlocking the chains on the brain."

Solomon believes that the elimination of Malcolm X caused many African Americans to remain in the dark, their minds shackled and their potential cut off. His assassination left the community in a state of degradation. "Well, it was like it's all gone, it's all gone, you know. The course of Black America has changed."

Chapter 10: Solomon

The loss of Malcolm X was significant for Solomon, for Malcolm had become an internalized loved object. The experience of seeing Malcolm X in his casket during the documentary was a blow to his psyche. The pain of seeing his death unfold *even at a temporal and spatial distance* was unbearable. "It's like being robbed," Solomon explained. "You just got robbed, you got screwed again, raped. Somebody took something from you that you can never get back. It was taken, it's gone. And you'll never know how it would've played out."

As the interview continued, I noticed Solomon's defenses beginning to lower; he began to disclose the pain that he had buried for so long. Solomon began to search deeper within himself to express his feelings about the loss of the leaders:

> "Well, that's a violation, you've just been violated. And, okay, I can tell you. I know a feeling, and this is a very true feeling. It's like the feeling I had, and I got to understand that feeling for the second time in my life. The first time would have been with the whole Civil Rights Movement and the elimination of Martin Luther, of Malcolm X. But the feeling that I was able to associate with this came back to me when I got my first prostate exam. You feel totally violated. I don't know if you ever been through that. But it's that feeling, you know. I never understood what a woman would feel like being raped, but that first prostate exam, you know, it's this total violation.... I mean, it's something that's happened to you. It's been taken from you or done to you and you didn't appreciate it at all, but it just happened, you know. In the case of the prostate exam, at least you know it was necessary, and

you submitted. But you didn't like it, and it
had to happen, and you know it's the only way.
It's got to happen, but man, this is terrible. I
just feel so bad."

The loss of the civil rights leaders disrupted the unity and
resiliency of the African American community. While
resiliency may still exist in some pockets, the overall unity
has been greatly disturbed. Historically Blacks have felt uneasy
in America, but the problems and struggles of the past
crystallized into a desire to work together against the common
foe. With the murder of the internalized loved objects
(leaders), the fear of death has also been internalized. Solomon
says,

"I mean, we were in the projects, we were in
the Robert Taylor Homes. You know the
Robert Taylor Homes? We were in the Robert
Taylor Homes in '68. My exact memory
without really understanding what was going
on, every night I could look out the window
on the 10th floor of 5266 South State, I could
look out my bedroom window and see lines
of paddy wagons throwing brothers in the back
of the truck, beating them, throwing them in
the back of the truck. That's my first, that's
my oldest memory. I didn't really understand
what was going on, but that was about the Civil
Rights Movement."

The torture and degradation of African Americans were
addressed by the leaders. In the midst of hostility, the leaders
gave the community hope. While the leaders lived, the Black

community was provided support from within. However, today, Solomon says that

> "We have no unity, especially in the lower socio-economic sectors. But it's probably not true especially in the lower economic social sector. It's probably true across the whole spectrum, because when you get up in corporate, you know, we have no unity. Our biggest adversary would be another Black person."

Within the context of Black disunity, the function of the leaders today is to pacify the community with magical and wishful thinking. Solomon adds, "And because of the effects of all the things that Black America has seen to this day, [the leader] wouldn't get it. He wouldn't get that support from his people. They're all about themselves, and for different reasons, you know."

Solomon's reflections make me realize more than ever that psychological reparation is the path to healing. Yes, it is painful, but processing through the grief rather than burying it frees the soul. When the soul of the community is freed from the phantasies, the magical thinking, the manic defenses, then we will clearly see the true colors of our "leaders." Only then will we begin to demand responsibility and accountability from our leaders and organizations.

Chapter 11: Loretta

Loretta's interview was held at a local restaurant. She indicated that she would be more comfortable expressing herself in a social setting.

Loretta was a child during the Civil Rights Movement. I guess most women, or people in general, do not want to be considered old. As we began the interview, she clearly expressed that she was not an active participant during the movement and that she was only a child. She stated, "Like I said, civil rights, that was a little bit before my time. I can talk a little about post-civil rights." Her statement is significant because it demonstrates the impact of the movement, not only on those who participated in the marches, boycotts, and protests, but also on later generations.

Still, Loretta feels connected in a significant way to the leaders of the movement. "I want to say, part of my inspiration was one of my uncles who was actually a friend of Fred Hampton." Fred Hampton was the leader of the Illinois branch of the Black Panther Party. Loretta was not certain if her uncle was a member of the Black Panther Party, but she identified with the Black Panthers in a way that resembles internalization:

> "I felt, I looked at them, I thought they were like my big brothers or something.... My uncle threw a party, and a lot of his Panther friends came by. It was like they're all like these big big brothers or uncles or whatever you want to call them."

Loretta felt protected by the Panthers. Given her description of them as uncles or big brothers, it is clear that she had internalized them as loved objects. She added, "Like

I said, they had that big brother/uncle-type aura about them."
Webster's New Collegiate Dictionary defines *aura* as "a subtle
sensory stimulus" or "a distinctive atmosphere surrounding a
given source." Something within Loretta connected to these
men. She perceived them as good and powerful.

If the dismantling of the Black Panther Party affected the
Black community, Loretta, who knew some of them
personally, must have felt the loss in her soul. Yet when I
asked her about it she only said, "Now when you think of it,
yeah, that is missing. It is a little disconcerting because some
of these young folks don't have an identity."

Loretta acknowledges the empty space, the something that
is missing from the community. Unofficially she speaks for
young people who "don't have an identity." The Black
Panthers identified with the people; in doing so they gave the
community an identity. When the identifiers were removed,
so was the identity.

Loretta was only five or six when Fred Hampton was
assassinated. She remembers being "shocked." She couldn't
believe what had happened. "It's kind of like with the Malcolm
thing, you know. Once again they gun down someone who
has the definite potential to make a difference in people's lives.
They like to get them young so they wouldn't be around too
long."

Loretta was disappointed at what happened, but during
the interview, she expressed little emotion. The purpose of
defense mechanisms is to prevent the experience of pain. I
believe Loretta's flat responses indicated a manic defense
against feeling the loss of her "big big brothers." After being
asked questions about the assassinated civil rights leader who
was connected to a member of her family, she stated, "You
like to ask a lot of these emotional questions, but sometimes
I don't always react, you know. I try to keep emotions out
of it."

Chapter 11: Loretta

I asked her how the deaths of other civil rights leaders had affected her. Again, she stated that she was disappointed:

> "You know, a lot of time, as a people, we can be very emotional. That's why I say, when you get too emotional you don't think clearly, and you forget, you don't see the whole picture. That's why sometimes you just got to—yeah, I know it breaks your heart to see this happening. But sometimes you gonna have to take some breaths, calm down, and try to pull all the pieces together."

As a young child she may not have been able to process such tremendous grief properly. Erecting defenses is the psyche's way of providing protection from pain. As Loretta stated, "Yeah, at first I was probably emotional, but then I have to put it in perspective."

Loretta shared her observations of the Black community post-civil rights. She's clearly aware of the void created by the loss of the civil rights leaders and organizations. She stated, "They don't want us getting in control. They don't want us loving ourselves. They want us to stay, like, in the state of mind of unawareness, like we are. They want us to keep on having no identity."

Loretta expresses anger when I ask her about the condition of the community and especially the loss of courage within. Note her halting speech in the following quote. My questions have begun to reach a deeper place within her soul.

> "Because it seems like every time, you know, someone even remotely, you know, gets there then some mysteriously off'd out.... One person that I can think of offhand is maybe Tupac. But he didn't even get—I don't even

know how far he was going or where he was getting before, you know, he was gunned down. But you gotta see. It's always someone young, a younger person. Just like with Fred Hampton, you know, only 21. So people don't want to take any chances."

Fearfulness has replaced courageous advocacy. On a daily basis the community lives with paralyzing fear. The loss of the leaders removed from the community the courage and motivation to face death. Today, the community exists without this model of courage. Loretta stated,

"Well I think, you know, after, you know, somebody, you know, gets up there and tries to be the voice of the people and they've been gunned down they just figure, oh, okay, well, you know, you get somebody here and then all they gone do is just murder them."

As long as the community is held hostage by fear, any new leaders will be stifled and controlled by this fear. This fear has essentially disabled the community's desire to improve. Loretta states, "But I think another part of the problem is, you know, a lot of us, you know, have just given up, you know. You have a leader or someone who's been effective over the years and then, you know, he's gunned down or something like that, okay."

Fear has eroded the community's memory of the good work done by the civil rights leaders and organizations. Fear does not remove the threat of danger, but it removes the objective of those who faced the danger. To remember the leaders would bring pain and a challenge to repair. In the words of Yoda the fictional mentor/instructor in several *Star Wars* films, "Fear is the path to the dark side. Fear leads to anger. Anger leads to hate. Hate leads to suffering."

Chapter 12: Malik

Malik began the interview by disclosing that he is the parent of a crime victim. His daughter was shot and died in the midst of a shootout in a Black neighborhood. That tragedy motivated him to become involved with community groups.

As the discussion led to the Civil Rights Movement and the leaders of the movement, Malik indicated that Malcolm X was a significant leader for him.

> "The thing about Malcolm, he was a Black leader that people could identify with…. Back then, leaders like Malcolm 'nem was in the community, and people had a choice. They could touch you…. They was in the community, motivating, you know."

Malik was impressed with the civil rights leaders. He felt that they were accessible and physically present within the community. Malik said that he was inspired by Malcolm X. "You can look at a man like Malcolm and say, 'Wow! That's how I should be.' That's how I want to be, you know. That's what inspired me."

Malcolm X was Malik's source of strength and model of confidence. He liked Malcolm's belief in unity. He fulfilled a role within the Black community that was significant and awesome. Malik stated, "His role was getting the community united and showing young Black men that you can be somebody, that you can stand up, and that you can hold your head high."

Malik's knowledge and contact with Malcolm X was through the media, for example, documentaries and the movie *Malcolm X* by Spike Lee. When he saw the image of Malcolm X, something connected within him. The internal connected with the external. His reaction to the presence of Malcolm X was

> "Man, powerful. You look at that and say, that's power. That's power when you can move and motivate people, and not through fear, but through inspiring people…. You look at some of these old reels and some of that carried over, that feeling that carried over into the '70s when we was growing up. It was the community."

Malik believes that Malcolm X is a model for Black men today. Malik was impressed when he learned of Malcolm's history. It created a strong desire and motivation within him to do good in the community. "His transformation from what he *was* into who he *became*, see, that's what's powerful about Malcolm—who he was and what he became. Because a lot of people can relate to that story. You can relate to him."

Malik admired Malcolm's style of leadership. He believes that if Malcolm X were alive today he would make a significant impact within the Black community. He stated, "If he could do it then, he can do it now."

Although he never knew Malcolm personally, Malik's statements suggest that he has internalized the great leader into his inner world. The physical Malcolm is not available, but his strong psyche or soul helps Malik share in Malcolm's vision.

> "You wish you had that kind of leadership. It just seemed real, it didn't seem phony. It didn't seem like they had hidden agendas. That was their agenda, to make the Black community better. Their agenda wasn't trying to get a bigger church or trying to get this or trying to get that. Their agenda was the Black community. And that's what's missing."

Chapter 12: Malik

When talking about Malcolm X, Malik spoke with zeal and enthusiasm. The discussion had a life of its own, fueled by his admiration. For Malik, Malcolm X was the perfect leader for the Black community. However, he also respects the courage of Dr. King.

> "But you don't know enough to get personal until you see what those men really stood for, and you be like, wow! You know what I'm saying? Could you do what they did under the pressure that they were under? They were some real leaders. Man, if you got some leaders like that today, man, I believe people will follow."

Malik credited Malcolm X for bringing unity to the community. He stated, "That word don't really exist no more. That word *community*." With the loss of Malcolm, an empty space was created.

> "Oh, it's always something missing, you know. For instance, like we're talking about Fred Hampton. Fred was a big influence, but yeah, it's always something missing. When you've got leaders missing from the community you are going to have a void. A void with young Black men, you know. You want to blame a lot of these young Black guys, men, because they angry, because they don't know.... We got a lot missing. And, yes, like I said, it affects me just like I see it affects a lot of young people."

Malik talked about anger, his own and the community's, at the loss of the leaders.

"But it do kind of piss you off *(laugh)*, you know what I'm saying? It does kind of piss you off. And that's why we have a lot of angry young men. They angry, people are angry for a reason. You look at where we probably could have been from what they started to build. If it kept going upward and building, imagine where the community would be at today if the stepping stones kept going higher and higher."

Losing a loved object is difficult. Malik learned about Malcolm's assassination through the media. He stated, "You felt hurt by it, yeah."

Malik's reaction to the loss of Malcolm X was full of frustration.

"Man, that's progress stopped.... You take the leadership, you got a lot of followers running around, a lot of soldiers running around with no guidance. You know, we'll give you a day and build that statue, but your movement has stopped, you know."

Following the demise of the civil rights era, many Black leaders rose up in government, education, business, the community, and the church. Malik stated, "To me, true Black leaders don't really exist today." Malik's statement is based on his involvement with church leaders, community activists, and other post-civil rights leaders.

"To be honest, to me, like I said, this is my own personal opinion, could be wrong, it's just my opinion, man, but to me, we don't have true Black leaders anymore. That's why they ain't in the hood.... These Black so-called civil rights leaders, where you at? And then they want to blame people for not coming to them. You the leaders, you supposed to come to me! You supposed to be in the community, you supposed to be making a difference, and you supposed to be out here talking to these so-called gang leaders. The people that have the influence got to be the ones that lead, and they ain't doing that."

Corruption and ineffectiveness among leadership are examples of manic reparation. Today's leaders have not shown the community how to mourn and learn from the loss of the civil rights leaders. The emptiness must be acknowledged so that the community can be put on the right path once again.

"Are you willing to be brave enough to do what those leaders did back then? All those leaders that gave their lives to make it better, you know. A lot, some of these leaders, they either sold out because they getting so much money from the government, funding they programs, you know. It's like the government in they pocket. You only can do so much. You can't do what they don't allow you to do. That's what it seems like now. You got all these TV leaders, you know. What pisses me off is, just like they pick and choose when these kids get killed...whenever the TV cameras show up, that's when the Black so-called leaders show up. But when the cameras go away, they disappear. We got a lot of leaders like that today. They want the status of a Malcolm and a Martin, but they don't want to put on the line what those men put on the line. That's how I honestly feel, you know. When things happen, even a lot of these pastors, they get on TV, they talk all this crap, but when the TV cameras go away, you don't see them. Just like I said, we got all these organizations, but it's like people are not working together. I mean, where is the real unity?"

Malik discussed his anger at the loss of the Black leaders and the refusal of the new leaders to show courage, to put their lives on the line for the sake of the community, to acknowledge the loss of the civil rights leaders. At least Malik is able to express his anger while stuck in his pain. So many in the community feel like Malik, full of anger and frustration at the substandard conditions in the community but confused about what to do. Many have a ferocious desire to repair the conditions, but without processing through the pain, they will stay stuck in the vicious cycle of their anger.

Chapter 13: Kareema

Kareema wanted to have her interview in her office. She was eager and informative throughout the meeting. Kareema was not an active participant during the Civil Rights Movement, but she has been engaged with community programs and groups that are directly related to the civil rights leaders and organizations.

Kareema is very fond of the Black Panther Party. When she saw the Panthers as a girl, she felt proud, empowered, and safe. She was

> "…proud that Black men had the courage to speak and be visible about their concerns, that they was strong, to stand up and speak for themselves…. If we band together, that's how we become powerful, and we are a powerful people when we can come together."

Kareema holds men in high regard. The Black Panthers represented for her the ideal man, and she was inspired by this group of Black men.

> "I grew up believing that when you have a man supporting you, he's there to protect you. So if you have these group of Black men, you can feel safe because they gone protect you. If something go down, as we say, you can feel safe because you know that they got your back."

Kareema internalized the Panthers as father figures who protected and provided safety for the community. She believes that if the Black Panther Party were more active today, they would be able to resolve the issues of the Black community.

> "We wouldn't see the devastation at the level that we see now in our community…. Like you say, there are still some members, but if the movement was still prevalent, our educational system would be much, much better than it is now. Our jails wouldn't be filled with young men because they would be in those apprenticeship programs. They would be learning skills that would help them get a job. So they wouldn't have the drugs in the community because we wouldn't allow it to be in the community."

Kareema felt that the Black Panther Party held the community together. During the civil rights era, the Panthers gave the Black community empowerment and a sense of purpose.

Kareema also credits the Black Panthers with educating the Black community.

> "So when we were no longer in physical constraints, the Black Panther movement was able to…unchain the minds. That was something they were afraid of 'cause they say, aw man, if they minds get unchained, we in trouble. So we gonna have to do something about this, you know, to stop it 'cause we don't want them *(laugh)* around basically."

Kareema presents the Panthers as a loved object of the community and a threat to the racist Whites of America. The

Chapter 13: Kareema

Panthers helped free Blacks from a status of inferiority. They unified the community with direction and purpose.

When I asked Kareema about the demise of the Black Panther Party, she said the racist Whites of America

> "...don't want to give up their piece of pie. So they did what came natural to them and that was to destroy that movement. I just feel sad because we live in a country that does that, and then it doesn't bother us that we live in a country that does *(laugh)* things like that. You understand what I'm saying?"

As Kareema talked about the loss of the Black Panthers, she expressed sadness. I sensed that this sadness had been present within her long before the interview, possibly even as long ago as her childhood when the loved object (Black Panther Party) had been dismantled. She also felt sadness over the loss of Dr. King.

> "It's sad because Black people, well, in my experience, seem to be easily intimidated. Seem like we should have been in an uproar when that happened. I mean, we should have really been tearing this country up left to right. Because if you truly believe in what he stood for, and you know what King stood for, it's no way, 40 years later, we should be in the condition that we're in. So that's what makes me sad about. It's like, all the hard work he did and all the lives people lost. He lost his life, you know, and his family suffered. All of that just makes me sad that we just not doing what we supposed to do."

Kareema believes that fear is exacerbating the community's stagnation.

> "I know that's probably what a lot of people fear, because it has happened with King, and it happened with Malcolm, and it happened with Fred. I'm sure in the back of a lot of people mind…it could happen with me if I stand up and say something that somebody doesn't like—especially the government. They don't like this, they gone put a hit out on me or my family or whatever. 'Cause don't nobody want to lose they life. Everybody fearful…. I think that's what broke it up. It's people just being fearful because it takes a strong and courageous person to do what Martin did, and do what Malcolm, and do what Fred. And see, that's just three out of millions of Blacks that we have in this country."

Kareema's view of the post-civil rights leaders moved her from sadness to anger. (Sadness is more towards the healing depressive position while anger develops the manic defense.) She believes that elected officials are the new leaders today. Kareema expressed her frustration at the officials' lack of concern. She was

> "…frustrated because again, like I said, we have a lot of Black leaders, I mean Black officials with position, and it makes me frustrated because they are comfortable and careful to sit back and not try to do the things that they really could do…. It angers me because they're not concerned with human life. Where did we lose that?"

Chapter 13: Kareema

Kareema connects the end of the movement with the crises of today. In her sadness, she experiences and begins to process the pain of the community, but then her anger and frustration toward Black leaders rise up. This going back and forth between true psychological reparation and manic reparation is prevalent throughout the community.

However, there's hope in Kareema's ability to embrace the loss of the Black Panther Party. Her sadness could lead to healing and growth. She said, "It's just allowed me to continue to think about the role that I play in the community and how I can further educate and prepare myself so that I can definitely call myself a Black Panther member one day *(laugh)*, you know."

Chapter 14: Latifah

Latifah is an educator and activist in the inner city. Of all the participants, she was the farthest removed from the Civil Rights Movement, having been born after the movement ended. Her knowledge of the movement is through first- and secondhand sources.

> "I think that first image I probably ever really saw, I was fortunate that my mother would give me these little books. I don't know where she got them from, but they'd be just four-page books about a different African American in history, whatever the case, and I'd never seen it all put together until I saw the *Eyes on the Prize* [TV] series when I was, like, 10 or 11."

Latifah is a community activist with Reverend Jesse Jackson and his community action programs. She participates in marches and demonstrations for community improvement. Latifah acknowledges that her active involvement with Jesse Jackson enhances her awareness of the Civil Rights Movement.

> "Through that, I became more cognizant of my past and more cognizant of how all of his efforts continue and why they continue and how there is still so much work to be done. So that kind of puts me at an advantage compared to most people my age who only sit on the periphery of a civil rights experience."

Although Latifah is very active with Jesse Jackson and his programs, the Black Panther Party made an even greater impact within her. She stated that she was enthralled and intrigued by the Black Panther movement, so the loss of some party members due to assassination, silencing, and imprisonment has been a great disappointment. Latifah stated,

> "Bobby Seale is making barbecue cookbooks! Like, are you serious? Come on! I used to idolize you, and you're talking about ribs? Are you serious? No!.... Even in your later years you still have an opportunity to go back and teach, and I mean literally in the classroom."

Her activism has given her a clear perspective of how the community sank into the manic defense of capitalism and individualism post-civil rights.

> "That's another reason why my generation suffers so sorely. Our parents are trying to escape the memories. And so they didn't tell us, and they didn't tell us in detail, and they purposely didn't tell us, and all they told us was, get out here. Get your money. Do what's right for you and yours. Be quiet. Have a nice house. Don't bother anyone. That is the sum of your life."

As Latifah stated, the manic defenses of capitalism—getting paid, going into debt, buying big houses, etc.—oppose the vision of the Civil Rights Movement for Black America.

Without her activism, Latifah might have gotten caught up in anger and frustration (manic reparation). And while Latifah does experience anger and frustration from time to time, for the most part she has transformed her own manic defenses by studying civil rights, becoming a community activist, and working through the sadness.

Chapter 15: Leroy

Leroy experienced integration during the civil rights era when his parents moved his family into a predominantly White neighborhood. He stated, "They did so explicitly to get us into the better school system, and this was in the '60s."

Leroy's parents were actively involved in the Civil Rights Movement and believed in the concept of integration.

> "You all start to realize that I grew up during the time of Martin Luther King and Malcolm X. And I listened to Malcolm X talk on the radio, read some of his stuff when I was in middle school and high school, and there were parts of what he said that I agree with, parts of what he said I didn't agree with. The self-sufficiency piece, no problem with that at all. Make your way in the world making decisions, taking personal responsibilities. I agree with that. But the segregationist rhetoric, the violent rhetoric, no, I didn't buy into that at all."

As did many intellectuals of the Civil Rights Movement, Leroy listened to both positions. His parents were supporters of Dr. King, and other family members supported Malcolm X and the Black Panther Party.

> "So I have these crosscurrents in my family the entire time I was growing up. I had to develop my own identity during the '60s. I had to figure out what's come over me, what works for me. And so, me, I'd lean heavily toward Martin Luther King because he came under the Gandhi tradition of nonviolence and

inclusion. And that was basically what I heard from my parents."

Leroy internalized Dr. King as a significant loved object. He was able to internalize both his parents' expectations and Dr. King's philosophy within himself.

> "It was really good because he was an intellectual. Because he knew how to talk, and one of the things that my parents stressed to us in our house when we were growing up is the use of proper English.... So seeing Martin Luther King on TV, he was an intellectual. He knew how to talk. He knew how to use the language. He could give a speech that would keep you enthralled, and he would do so in a language of the dominant society."

Every aspect of Dr. King served as a model of manhood and activism for Leroy.

> "I was a real driven person in respect to that. And a lot of that has to do with what I saw from Dr. King and the message that he was preaching. It said go out there into that world and prepare yourself academically and intellectually prepare yourself because your place at the table is coming. And I believed in that rhetoric."

After the assassination of Dr. King, Leroy

> "...wondered whether or not the movement [would] continue. Because one of the things that has been both our strength and our

weakness in the African American community is that we tend to crystallize ourselves around one person who then becomes the spokesman for the entire community. And so the worries and fears of the African Americans were, Dr. King is dead. Who was going to take on the mantle? Who's going to do this?"

Since the loss of Dr. King, Leroy believes that the community has existed without guidance or direction.

"See, I think that with the…diversity of opinions out there, it's hard to coalesce people around a movement…today than it was 40 years ago. Because they can see African Americans here, they are everywhere in the society. Before you didn't see that. Everybody was inside the same bubble. So I think in that respect it makes it difficult…. But I don't see the fervor or the willingness to engage as much as I saw back in the '60s."

Leroy says the community is fragmenting for the purpose of advancement and opportunities. The problems within the community were magnified as a result of the good being separated from the bad. The loss of the civil rights leaders caused both viewpoints to be without guidance and leadership.

Leroy used the phrase "unintended consequences" during his interview. One of the unintended consequences of the Civil Rights Movement was the successful integration of communities. Middle-class working families were able to leave the segregated community. As a large segment of educated African Americans left the Black community for the suburbs, crime appeared to increase in the inner city. Leroy talked about the overwhelming presence of crime, violence, and self-hatred in the community. While the leaders promote peace, love, and unity, hatred flourishes.

> "What's changed is that a significant chunk of the African American community has moved away. That's changed. The projects have always been there. The projects ain't going anywhere. They've always been there. And because of that, those attitudes, those beliefs get…transmitted on to subsequent generations. I mean, that hasn't changed at all. You hear people referred to as [having] a ghetto mentality, whatever you want to call it, a project mentality, a barrio mentality, or Indian Reservation mentality. Any time circumstances in a particular area don't change over time, people's beliefs and attitudes and mentality are not going to change. What's happened is, particularly in African American communities, is that a large chunk, that is, the middle class who had to stay in this community because they were largely segregated by law, no longer live there. That's changed. And so what you get left with is the bottom of the economic barrel. And that sort of perpetuates itself over time."

Thus, not only has poor leadership created a crisis in the community, but so has the drain of the educated Black middle class from Black neighborhoods. According to Leroy, the void in the community appears to have been created by two events: the absence of the civil rights leaders and the absence of the community.

Chapter 16: Syrus

Syrus was a participant in the 1995 Million Man March that was organized by the Nation of Islam. The march was a modern day demonstration focusing more on what Blacks needed to do for themselves rather than what the government would not do for the community. Syrus stated:

> "The cause of the Million Man March was something that appealed to me personally.... One of the causes that was articulated was the recognition that Black families, but Black men in particular, had a difficult life experience here in this country. Because of that experience we had internalized a number of things.... [We] lost our footing or our place in not only how we dealt with racism and the other issues of the world but even how we dealt with our own families and how we were responsible."

Syrus' statement speaks directly to the internalization of the community's experience. He identifies the state of being "lost" within the community. The civil rights leaders were guides, gatekeepers, and protectors who enlightened and nurtured the community. Dr. King was the leader who most influenced Syrus. He internalized Dr. King as a significant loved object and role model.

> "Well, you have to be convicted to do the right thing and be a leader and [stick] with your convictions and maintain your integrity. That's what I see a lot with Dr. King. It's really all that you have. Sometimes it takes courage to do that. But you can build off other people

you've seen that came before you to do that. So when I think about [it], that's the closest thing I can equate to even my own lifestyle."

The assassination of Dr. King left a great emptiness within Syrus.

"Well, it's anger for sure, for certain. I can really recall, especially during my college years, I think by the time I hit 19, 20s in college—I can really remember understanding around the time when we celebrate his birthday every year. Really understanding the impact of his death. Being angry about the fact that he had to die at 39, sacrificed his life for his people…. Just having a real anger for that. When you look at the hypocrisy of it all, why would people have to die when the so-called forefathers of the same country within the Declaration of Independence and the Pledge of Allegiance, all of these other identifiers with the country that talked about freedom and liberty and justice for all, and then recognizing that it was just a lie for our people? And then our people had to give up the ultimate sacrifice just to fight to have the opportunity for it."

Today's leaders attempt to address the loss of the civil rights leaders without showing us how to endure and transform the pain of the loss. This failure to deal with suffering has led to the manic defense of opportunism among our leaders today.

"Well, I think a lot of it is just self-interests. I think we don't have the caliber people now, or not to the magnitude of them that were

willing to sacrifice their very life for the
people. Like Martin Luther King, they put their
life on the line. We don't do that anymore, you
know. We don't have people that do that. Some
so-called leaders now won't come out unless
they get an honorarium. So it's not even about
putting their life on the line, you know. If
they're not getting paid they're not coming
out."

Syrus believes that the civil rights leaders would have
combated the tremendous destruction that is occurring today
from drugs, crime, lack of education, and socioeconomic
exploitation.

"Absolutely, yeah absolutely. Because, see, the
civil rights leaders at the time were good. They
met any issue that was an issue. They were
dealing with all the various issues, right?
Economics, violence, fighting against the
schools, the inequities of the schools, whatever
the issues. So to me, the drug situation would
have been no different. I can't see them sitting
on the sideline and not try to get people
organized to deal with that."

Syrus disclosed some of the manic defenses, the ways we
avoid pain, that he and the community shares.

"You've just got to move forward. But you
know, I think for all Black people, for us in
particular, it's always kind of below the
surface, not far below the surface. And that's

another thing that we struggled with a lot—
the violence in our neighborhoods and even it
is not violence, and not the stored resentment,
and health. The things that are born out of our
health: heart attacks and the stresses and all of
that. I think a lot of that is just dealt with
internalizing a lot of the anger that we haven't
been able to deal with because of our
experiences."

As Syrus states, we have created manic defenses to deal
with our painful life experiences. His summation neatly
describes the essence of post-civil rights manic reparation in
the African American community.

"Another negative byproduct of our experience
is that [we Black men] don't talk through our
experiences. We don't have that whole, what
is it, the catharsis kind of experience. Because
we don't talk to [anyone], we just internalize
it as we kill, and we let it kill us or we kill
somebody. We don't talk to [anyone]. So this
is just a great opportunity for me personally.
Because it's almost like a real self-discovery
and talking through it and connecting with
thoughts and feelings that are really real.
Without having this conversation, just really
haven't thought a whole lot about."

True reparation will begin for the community when
African Americans become aware of how their manic defenses
block the pain of the loss and prevent growth and wholeness.
Until then, manic reparation will continue to cycle in various
forms throughout the community.

Chapter 17: Joseph

Joseph actively participated in civil rights marches led by Dr. Martin Luther King, Jr.

> "I had this experience with the movement ever since 19, I guess. If I had to officially give a time for my direct involvement in the Civil Rights Movement it would probably be 1955, the beginning of the Montgomery boycott. But even before that, August of 1955. I would have been 14 years of age, I believe. The death of Emmett Till struck me in such a way that I am kind of constantly reminded of his death every day."

Dr. King was a great influence on Joseph. Practically every aspect of Dr. King resonated with Joseph, and he internalized him as a significant loved object. Joseph stated, "I think Dr. King was one of the greatest human beings I've ever met."

Dr. King was accessible to the community, and Joseph met him at an early age.

> "I was just meeting a man by the name of Dr. King. I was impressed, to be very honest about it. I was in eighth grade when I first met him, and he came to a career day. What I was impressed with was that here was a young man who was 25 or 26; I think he might have been 26, and had his PhD from Boston....
>
> "When I first met Dr. King, it was just like any other individual. You saw him, you spoke to him, and he saw you, he spoke to you. And

then along came the Montgomery boycott ....
What really impressed me, he didn't have to
do this.... It still impress[es] me to this day,
what he has done for this country."

The personality, activism, and courage of Dr. King
influenced Joseph's ideas, goals, and perspective. In a somber
voice Joseph stated,

> "I wish I could be more like him. I wish I had
> the articulation that he had. I appreciated how
> humble he was. He was not caught up in the,
> what do you call it, the group sort of speak.
> His humility really impressed me. He didn't
> have the entourage; you know what I mean....
> Later in his life they really had to protect him.
> You can see Dr. King just walking down the
> street by himself. And when you look at the
> impact he had, you know, you would think he
> had the big head. I've never got that
> impression. I just thought that was an
> outstanding tribute to a human being who
> really had the world watching him.... I still
> honor that. I wish I could be as humble as he
> was."

The assassination of Dr. King was a tremendous blow to
Joseph. The loss of a significant loved object who serves as a
paragon of one's hopes and dreams creates a devastating
emotional response. Joseph stated, "So sorry that he left so
early. I think it would've been a much better world. And
saddened today that many children, specifically Black
children, don't even know who Dr. King is."

Chapter 17: Joseph

Joseph recalled the day of Dr. King's assassination.

> "It was on a Friday, I believe it was. I don't
> know why I was home that day? I remember
> being in the middle of the bed for some reason.
> You know how you're asleep and you hear
> something and you wake up? There was a
> bulletin, you know, Dr. King had been shot. I
> knew he was dead then. *(In a very soft voice)*
> I just knew he was dead. For some reason I
> knew he was dead.... Oh yeah, I remember
> that day."

Joseph had such a deep connection to Dr. King that he
had a "gut feeling" when Dr. King was shot. Joseph began
the initial stage of true reparation, but the pain apparently
proved to be unbearable.

> "I guess it was much more sorrow and, you
> know, why did it happen to him and *(laugh)*
> why didn't it happen to someone else? I don't
> think I was, I guess I was angry, but I was under
> control about the way I thought about things. I
> didn't feel like I should go out and riot and
> break somebody's windows. I just thought that
> it was a tragedy that we were trashing our own
> neighborhoods. And so it was a time of
> reflection, and where do we go from here?"

A significant loved object for Joseph was killed. Joseph
acknowledged that there is, to this day, emptiness within him.
Joseph stated, "I guess any time something like that happens
there is a certain amount of emptiness. But life goes on.... I
didn't feel like going out and killing White people. I didn't
feel any of that stuff."

Chapter 18: Final Analysis

"You can kiss your family and friends good-
bye and put miles between you, but at the same
time you carry them with you in your heart,
your mind, your stomach, because you do not
just live in a world but a world lives in you."
— Frederick Buechner (1977, p. 3)

In this chapter I will present the themes that emerged from the interviews in a way that will promote an understanding of the phenomena studied (Golafshani, 2003), namely, the need for psychological reparation in the African American community. The participants generously shared their insights about the challenges facing the community and the breakdown of the community after the Civil Rights Movement. The value of their contribution to this study is the fact that these insights come from their years of community activism, of working directly with African Americans who have been harmed by the disintegration of the community.

The raw data of the participants' responses were tabulated and organized into 65 categories. These categories were distilled into the following six codes:

- Community Experience
- Continuing the Movement
- Post-Civil Rights Leaders
- Influence of the Civil Rights Leaders
- Manic Defenses within the Community
- Response to the Loss of the Leaders.

Community Experience – the situational reality of the community before and after the movement. For example, Kareema talked about substandard education:

"Look at our education system. Anywhere you
see a high population of Black children, they
got the poorest education system. They have

overcrowding of their classrooms, and they
don't have materials, things that was the same
thing that people of the Civil Rights Movement
was fighting and speaking against, you know."

Continuing the Movement – the participants' experiences
and apprehensions regarding the renewal of the movement.
Latifah wondered if we were even ready to move forward:

> "The fact that Dr. King was killed, the fact
> that COINTELPRO wiped out the Black
> Panther movement, every effort has been
> demolished, even down to the mysterious
> death of Harold Washington. All of that has
> deterred this generation. They think, as soon
> as we try, there will be consequences. Just even
> out of my own mouth, that, okay, we've got
> Obama, but he might get killed. This is our
> mentality. We think that for every effort that is
> made, there will be a counter-response. And
> some of us just aren't willing to stick our necks
> out like that."

Post-Civil Rights Leaders – information, perspectives,
or concerns about present-day ministers, politicians, and
community activists who are at the forefront of the community.
Most participants had doubts about the ability or desire of
today's leaders to fully commit to the struggle. As Syrus stated,

> "Well, I think a lot of it is just self-interests. I
> think we don't have the caliber people now,
> or not to the magnitude of them that were
> willing to sacrifice their very life for the
> people. Like Martin Luther King, they put their
> life on the line. We don't do that anymore, you

know. We don't have people that do that. Some so-called leaders now won't come out unless they get an honorarium. So it's not even about putting their life on the line, you know. If they're not getting paid they're not coming out."

Influence of the Civil Rights Leaders – the significance and internalization of the leaders as loved objects. As illustrated in the following comment by Joseph, loved objects of high caliber have the power to transform us:

> "I wish I could be more like him. I wish I had the articulation that he had. I appreciated how humble he was.... His humility really impressed me.... I am positive that I would not be doing what I am doing now had it not been for the influence of Dr. King. I am positive of that. I have no hesitation to tell anyone that Dr. King was an inspiration in my life, there's just no doubt.... But that inspiration, I'm sure, promoted by my family came from Dr. King. I mean, I'm just amazed by the man. He was amazing."

Manic Defenses within the Community – dominant emotions expressed by the community, including emptiness, sadness, and anger. Anger was the most common manic defense expressed, and this has been true of most of the community, post-civil rights. As a transformative agent, anger has a limited value. It only temporarily blocks the real pain of grief. As Malik stated,

> "But it do kind of piss you off *(laugh)*, you know what I'm saying? It does kind of piss you off. And that's why we have a lot of angry

young men. They angry, people are angry for a reason. You look at where we probably could have been from what they started to build. If it kept going upward and building, imagine where the community would be at today, if the stepping-stones kept going higher and higher.... Yeah, you get pissed off.... Hell yeah, it pisses you off."

Response to the Loss of the Leaders – manic defenses and the undermining of the community's positive transformation. Instead of continuing to fight for civil rights, the community has been on a path of destruction. This code is a pivotal mark in the study because it vividly illustrates the need for Kleinian psychological reparation. For example, regarding the loss of Malcolm X, Loretta stated, "Well I feel like we have to move on. We have to, uh, you know, you can't, he's gone. We need to look within our community and replace him. But that's a daunting task because of the damage that's been done."

One of the perceptions of manic reparation is that positive change is too daunting a task and thus must be avoided. Leroy stated,

> "See, I think that with the multiple of diversity of opinions out there, it's hard to coalesce people around a movement much more today than it was 40 years ago. Because they can see African Americans here, they are in everywhere in the society. Before you didn't see that. Everybody was inside the same bubble. So I think in that respect it makes it difficult—except for when there are certain hot button issues that occur. You can still get a protest if there is police brutality. You can still

get a protest if there is overt discrimination. Those things, you can still crystallize people around those issues."

Repeating Themes

Several repeating themes emerged from an analysis of the raw data, 65 categories, and six codes. The repeating themes had to be shared by at least two participants. The participants, who, remember, are also community activists, are not only working to improve the lives of African Americans, they are also wrestling with their own manic defenses of anger and grief. Thus the repeating themes that emerged from the individual interviews allow us to peer into the hearts and souls of the participants as well as the community. The repeating themes are as follows:

- The impact of slavery on the Black community post-civil rights
- The role of integration in the destruction of the Black community
- The ineffective presence of the church within the Black community
- The many challenges facing the Black community
- The unfinished work of the Civil Rights Movement

The impact of slavery on the Black community post-civil rights. Surprisingly, only three participants spoke about the impact of slavery. In addition to advocating for equal rights, the purpose of the movement was to foster an awareness of our history, including African civilizations and American slavery. This enhanced awareness developed mental fortitude, self-reliance, and self-worth. The fact that only three participants discussed the impact of slavery suggests an erosion of important knowledge in the community. Syrus said,

I think that we don't, as a people in particular, understand that we still are impacted by the experience of slavery and how it has been ingrained and inbred into our blood. Because, you know, that experience, I believe, had such a psychological impact that it's almost connected with your DNA…. If we're not real careful, we still act out many of the same behaviors that were prevalent during slavery as survival…. I could give you some very clear examples of that. One would be, you know, our mistrust of each other. I think a lot of that is because we can't explain it. A lot of us can't really explain why we have this inherent urge not to be supportive of each other, as Black people as a whole, devaluing each other. I think a lot of that came from just the experience of that whole experience of slavery and Jim Crow and Black people being degraded and devalued, and a lot of that we have internalized. We act it out. The killing of each other, seeing Black life not being as valued as White life. I think a lot of that is directly related to our experience, how we landed here and our early experience in this country."

The role of integration in the destruction of the Black community. The Civil Rights Movement wanted both: segregation and integration. Five of the participants spoke about integration and how it affected the community. Four of the five examined how integration damaged the community and the progress of the movement. Loretta talked about integration's role in the destruction of the community:

Chapter 18: Final Analysis

"It was destroyed along the way, especially with this integration. I think something happened along the way where people had a lot of thriving businesses back then. But I think somewhere along the way, somebody probably thought, you know, someone else's stuff was a little bit better or more on point than theirs. And so that kind of caused some sort of backslide with the businesses."

Loretta also spoke about moving beyond integration. She said, "There's a difference between integration and access. As a people do we really want to integrate, or [do] we just want access?"

However, only Leroy was in favor of integration:

"I was fortunate enough to have the opportunity to be raised in an integrated environment. And so I can have those attitudes, but what I was seeing going on around me, those things didn't connect. I grew up with White folks. I grew up with White folks that treated me respectfully."

The ineffective presence of the church within the Black community. The Civil Rights Movement was born in the Black church, yet two participants maintained that today's problems are related to a lack of church involvement. Joseph said,

"Well, I think there has been a breakdown in family values. When you have a breakdown in family values you talk about morals. The religious component of our community just seems not to be there…. I think our churches have not stepped up to bat…. Black churches have always been a powerful component of the Black community. We've got churches on every corner in Chicago, and the people are dying like flies."

Latifah said,

"The other contributing factor to that point is the fact that this generation isn't in the church the way that it used to be, and that's where people got the message. That's where people were able to galvanize. There is no meeting facility outside of the church in the Black community. There are places where we congregate and loiter *(laugh)*, but there are no other locations where you can go get information and strategize for a plan. The one thing that undergirded the Civil Rights Movement was that religious aspect.

"The only reason why the Nation of Islam was as strong as it was, or still is, is because of the religious element associated with it. And right now we have a society of wanderers who don't know God, who don't want to, and so they don't recognize that connection and that value and their accountability to one another."

The many challenges facing the Black community. All participants agreed that many challenges face the Black community. Many of the interviews focused on issues such as the breakdown of the family, poor education, substance abuse, violence, etc. They all addressed the destruction of the community post-civil rights. Syrus said,

> "Well, I think it's a combination of things. I think that because of the eroding of the Black family, not having leaders in many of these Black families, it fragmented...families and children in particular. And that had a devastating effect over all the Black community. And when you mix the introduction of illegal substances into our communities, I mean our communities were having a very tough time because of all the tenets of racism. You know, not having jobs and struggling to make ends meet. And then you had the eroding of the Black family. The last thing that needed to happen was introducing cocaine and crack cocaine and all of these substances in our neighborhoods.... I think what we're dealing with now is a destroyed community really based on, a large part, it's just the whole drug trade thing being introduced. And for people who may not think it's true, all you have to do, in my opinion, is look at what is the difference between 1975 and 1980. You look at the 1970s and the mid-1970s, Chicago in particular.... When you look at our toughest neighborhoods we just didn't have the level of violence. It...may have been interpersonal, you know, people who had domestic violence and other things. But if you look at 1980, right after drugs were really flooded, it was just totally different. And we've never stopped since then. The drug thing...has gotten us to where people don't even respect our Black elderly, you know. We at least at a time in the '70s respected our

elders, you know. But now we don't respect elders. We prey upon older Black people. They break in their houses and kill them and all of that. A lot of that was really the direct result of this drug thing, I believe. I think that was really intentional. I think that those that were the most corrupt and the most powerful in this country knew that a lot of money could be made off of drugs. And who were the least respected and endeared people in the country? That was the Black community. So drugs flooded right in our neighborhood."

Kareema said,

"The lack of jobs and a lack of education and a lack of guidance. These guys that are on the scene now, a lot of their dads are incarcerated, so they don't have any male mentors or male guidance. And like I say, the public officials, the politicians don't want to be bothered with them because they're not trying to make jobs available for them. They're not trying to do anything concerning the educational system and the laws that put them in jail in the first place, the drug laws or whatever. And then just allowing the drugs and stuff to come into our community, 'cause a man gotta work to eat, you know. So if it ain't no work, he gotta create work, and that's part of our history as being Black people. We gotta create, we've known to create work.... And then you know what drugs do to the mind, body, soul, and spirit. It corrupts the soul. That's what happens. So everybody out for themselves 'cause the effects of the drugs and the mentality. So you can't band together if you're high or under the influence or whatever."

Leroy held a perspective that was unexpected, different from the others, and added a twist to the hypothesis of this study:

> "Well, see to me that's never changed. That's not a progression at all. What's changed is that a significant chunk of the African American community has moved away. That's changed. The projects have always been there. The projects ain't going nowhere. They've always been there. And because of that, those attitudes, those beliefs get costly, transmitted on to subsequent generations. I mean, that hasn't changed at all.... Anytime circumstances in a particular area don't change over time, people's beliefs and attitudes and mentality are not going to change. What's happened is, particularly in African American communities, is that a large chunk, that is, the middle class who had to stay in this community because they were largely segregated by law, no longer live there. That's changed. And so what you get left with is the bottom of the economic barrel. And that sort of perpetuates itself over time."

The genius of the civil rights leaders was their ability to instill hope in the face of the many challenges facing the Black community. This was true leadership, something that is missing today—and the community suffers. Syrus reflected on the civil rights leaders' ability to create a new vision and instill hope:

"Absolutely, yeah absolutely. Because, see, the civil rights leaders at the time were good. They met any issue that was an issue. They were dealing with all the various issues, right? Economics, violence, fighting against the schools, the inequities of the schools, whatever the issues. So to me, the drug situation would have been no different. I can't see them sitting on the sideline and not try to get people organized to deal with that."

Malik said,

"You know what? I believe it would be some impact [from the civil rights leaders]. Because at the same time you got some people—I know some people myself, personally—that get high and would like to have a better way but don't know a better way. But if you got somebody showing you a better way, I believe it's a lot of people that would turn around. 'Say, man, I got to stop doing this, 'cause now I got some hope. I got something to live for. I'm a part of something positive, you know what I'm saying? I'm making a difference.'"

For the most part, the participants agreed: the decay of the Black community is a direct result of illegal drugs and "leaders" allowing the proliferation of crime and violence within the community.

The unfinished work of the Civil Rights Movement. Six of the eight participants discussed how the absence of committed civil rights leaders today has virtually halted progress in the Black community. Solomon stated,

"It slowed the movement down. Oh, had he been here we would be a lot further.... The longer he was here the quicker the movement progressed, I believe. Even though you might look back 40 years ago and say, well, we've come a long way, and, yeah, maybe we have, but we are not there yet. How much farther along would we be had Malcolm X still [been] here?"

Committed leaders are needed more than ever today. Latifah said, "So, when you look at patterns of discrimination in the housing market and you can pinpoint that African Americans, or people of color in general, were targeted for predatory loans, that lets you know that the movement isn't over." Joseph stated, "It's just kind of a permanent reminder to me of where we started and how far we've gone and still how far we have to go."

Six of the eight participants discussed how the assassination of the civil rights leaders affected the community's desire to continue the movement. Syrus stated, "Well, I think some people think it's going to jeopardize the little stuff that they have, you know. You got a job. You feel like if you say something you stand out. You're going to lose the little bit that you have." Kareema stated,

"I know that's probably what a lot of people fear because it has happened with King, and it happened with Malcolm, and it happened with Fred. I'm sure in the back of a lot of people's minds...it could happen with me if I stand up and say something that somebody don't like—especially the government. They don't like this, they gone put a hit out on me or my family or whatever."

Part 4: Our Future Hope

Chapter 19: Restoring the African American Mind

This study began by observing the Black community's experience post-civil rights and the need for psychological reparation. Any observer of the Black community in the 21st century would report increasing trauma. The Civil Rights Movement changed the psychology of Black America. The movement itself could be considered the birth of a nation. The cognitive behavioral psychologist may say that the core beliefs, the essence of what African Americans believe about themselves, had drastically changed.

The loss of the movement and its leaders is akin to the mother bird pushing the baby bird out of the nest. The bird must embrace the loss, endure the separation, and develop the ability to fly on its own all before hitting the earth. If a tree branch stops the fall and the bird floats to the ground, it may learn to walk but not fly. To learn how to fly, it must conquer the fear of falling. Manic reparation prevents true development and prevents the community from becoming whole.

The defenses of the community appear in many forms. These manic defenses lead to the following:
- Weak leaders whose only concern is self-gain
- Drug addiction, which serves as a buffer to prevent true psychological reparation
- Crime, which is an expression of both anger and emptiness.

Fear

Fear, the paranoid-schizoid position, is one of the major manic defenses expressed by the community. It has replaced the courage and boldness of the leaders and the movement. The community has become fearful of that which the movement stood against. This fear eats at the soul of the community and is passed on to subsequent generations. Continuing the progress of the movement and speaking with the boldness of the leaders terrify the community. This paranoia lingers within each generation of the Black community post-civil rights and is expressed both as paralysis and violence. Brian Daines (2000) said, "Unresolved loss can be passed on from the generation that directly experienced it to later ones both through individual and group processes."

Therefore, the community's paranoia serves as a defense against reparation. The reparation will be manic as long as the depressive position is avoided. As long as we refuse to mourn the loss of our leaders, the African American community will continue to fragment and digress. "Consequently, some losses can be worked through in a straightforward way by mourning, whereas others are complicated by ambivalence with resultant melancholia" (Daines, 2000).

The Value of Mourning

Daines (2000) wrote about the losses of World War I and how monuments and memorials were built and dedicated to help generations in their mourning process. Government holidays, huge sales, and athletic events all named after a slain civil rights leader is ludicrous, blasphemous, and far from the mourning and depressive processes which lead to reparation.

To embrace the pain and begin the process of reparation/ restoration, we can begin with the following:
1. Retrace, learn about, and embrace our history.
2. Acknowledge the accomplishments of the civil rights leaders.
3. Recall the progress of the community through their leadership, as well as what we lost at their demise.
4. Join active community organizations.

5. Decide that you want freedom, equality, and the right to live peaceably in this country—by any means necessary.
6. Love and respect Black people.
7. Support Black-owned businesses.
8. Become spiritually involved by renewing a relationship with God.

The Black Church

The community needs to process through its mourning, and the church can offer a form of group therapy. With the community in such a devastated state, churches should offer more than just good sermons on Sundays. The African American community needs to speak about the pain, and ministry should provide a safe environment to allow its members to be heard without judgment. African Americans need to talk about the pain and what it means to be Black in America. Growth and progress can then resume. The Black community can become respected on the soil where the blood of their ancestors was shed. Ultimately the community can celebrate one love.

Psychotherapy

Manic reparation is neither healthy nor productive for the African American community. The Black community has suffered throughout its existence in America. Laws have been passed, and the pain has been avoided; however, the residue of the suffering seems to linger and maintain its presence like the pink elephant in the conference room. While the pain is real and the hurt endures, no one has addressed the issue of this loss from a therapeutic perspective. Although African Americans tend not to get counseling, psychotherapy is exactly what is needed to process through the manic defenses of grief and anger. Syrus said,

> "Another negative byproduct of our experience is that [we Black men] don't talk through our experiences. We don't have that whole, what is it, the catharsis kind of experience. Because we don't talk to [anyone], we just internalize it as we kill, and we let it kill us, or we kill somebody. We don't talk to [anyone]. So this is just a great opportunity for me personally. Because it's almost like a real self-discovery and talking through it and connecting with thoughts and feelings that are really real. Without having this conversation, just really haven't thought a whole lot about."

Psychotherapy should be a strategy for healing in the community. Psychotherapy can facilitate "real self-discovery" and make the unconscious conscious by "talking through it and connecting with thoughts and feelings."

Although the Black community as a whole appears reluctant to get psychotherapy, the community can benefit and become whole through the therapeutic process. Without going into the recesses of the mind to unveil the trauma of slavery, the brutality of Jim Crow and the Civil Rights Movement, and the tragedies we experience today, the community cannot experience true reparation. Psychological reparation seeks to care for the soul. As prisons fill to capacity and new laws with even stricter penalties are being designed, we must urgently address the suffering that is hiding behind the violence, drug addiction, and rebellion. The psychotherapist's office is a safe space. We must take that first step—for the sake of our mental health, for the sake of the Black community, for the sake of America, for the sake of the world.

Group Gatherings

Community members should share thoughts and feelings in group gatherings to collectively experience and embrace the pain of Black history. During the interviews, Loretta said, "I think a lot of times it was too painful to discuss, but you know, it has to be discussed." Latifah said, "That's another reason why my generation suffers so sorely, because our parents are trying to escape the memories. And so they didn't tell us and they didn't tell us in detail, and they purposely didn't tell us...." The pain must be embraced for the community to develop as a whole and to move into the healing depressive position.

In South Africa, a strategic plan was developed to address the pain and suffering caused by apartheid. The Truth and Reconciliation Commission was formed. This is also needed in the African American community. Psychological reparation and social reparations must begin with knowing ourselves and all that has happened to us. When we know ourselves and honor our pain we can rise as a people, changed and matured by our experience. This will be our healing.

Epilogue

The Civil Rights Movement did not unfold in a closet. The movement was an American experience. Herein lies another piece to the puzzle.

The Civil Rights Movement involved many non-Blacks. Blacks, Whites, and those of other nationalities participated in the freedom rides, marches, and boycotts. What are the shared experiences of Whites and non-Blacks who supported the Civil Rights Movement? How did they feel about the loss of Dr. King and the Black Panther Party? The Black Panther Party also included non-Black members who were committed to the revolution.

As a Black man, I selfishly feel that the study of the Civil Rights Movement should focus on the Black phenomenon. However, America suffered from the loss of the Civil Rights Movement as well. Slavery, segregation, and racism are mental illnesses that America has placated for far too long. The symptoms have been given temporary relief, but the wound is still there. It hasn't been bandaged, but we're hoping it will heal anyway. Typically, when manic defenses can't be easily repaired, they are denied or disparaged. As we've learned from this study, any time a loss occurs, some discomfort will accompany the healing process.

At the end of each interview the participants were given the opportunity to express what the experience was like for them. Their responses were a plea for a therapeutic solution.

> *It is not that we can't progress. We won't progress. Our memories haunt us. Our collective experiences shelter us and overprotect us. Our phantasies shield us from making further progress towards our healing and what we need.*

Epilogue

The healing of Black America is not about receiving acceptance from White America. Rather it is about us accepting our own experience—the good, the bad, all of it: slavery, torture, lynchings, hatred, the multiple levels of abuse, and saying Never Again. We must accept our painful past and embrace the sorrow and mourning that it brings, and then when that depressive position has ripened and cured our soul, we can rise as a butterfly from its cocoon with a renewed sense of identity.

Black America

There exists inside of every descendant of slaves an emptiness, a hurt, a pain, a collective experience that wants to be acknowledged and properly mourned without the need to quickly move on, get over it, or merely accept it. We want to embrace the pain for as long as it takes. It will be worth it because now we understand: *the pain will birth the promise.*

"Harlem"

What happens to a dream deferred?

Does it dry up

Like a raisin in the sun?

Or fester like a sore—

And then run?

Does it stink like rotten meat?

Or crust and sugar over—

like a syrupy sweet?

Maybe it just sags

like a heavy load.

Or does it explode?

—Langston Hughes (1990, 1959)

References

Akbar, Na'im. 1991. *Visions for Black Men.* Nashville, TN: Winston-Derek Publishers.

Altman, Neil. 2005. "Manic Society: Toward the Depressive Position [Electronic version]." *Psychoanalytic Dialogues* 15 (3): 321-346.

Astor, James. 2002. "Analytical Psychology and Its Relation to Psychoanalysis: A Personal View [Electronic version]." *Journal of Analytical Psychology* 47:599-612.

Banks, William L. 2001. *The Case Against Black Reparation.* Haverford, PA: Infinity Publishing.

Baruch, Geoffrey. June 1997. "The Manic Defense in Analysis: The Creation of a False Narrative." *International Journal of Psychoanalysis* 78:549-559. http://search.ebscohost.com/login.aspx?direct=true&db=pph&AN=IJP.078. 0549A&site=ehost-live (retrieved March 29, 2008).

Bion, Wilford R. 1961. *Experiences in Groups, and Other Papers.* New York: Routledge.

Brandchaft, Bernard. 1986. "British Object Relations Theory and Self Psychology." *Progress in Self Psychology* 2:245-272. http://search.ebscohost.com/login.aspx?direct=true&db= pph&AN=PSP.002.0245A& site=ehost-live (retrieved March 29, 2008).

Brent, William Lee. 1996. *Long Time Gone.* New York: Times Books.

Buechner, Frederick. 1977. *Telling the Truth: The Gospel as Tragedy, Comedy, and Fairy Tale.* San Francisco: Harper & Row.

Burch, B. 1989. "Mourning and Failure to Mourn—An Object Relations View." *Contemporary Psychoanalysis* 25:608-623. http://search.ebscohost.com/login.aspx?direct=true&db=pph&AN=CPS.025.0608A&site=ehost-live (retrieved January 11, 2008).

References

Chafe, William H., et al, eds. 2001. *Remembering Jim Crow: African Americans Tell about Life in the Segregated South*. New York: The New Press.

Clarke, John Henrik. 1993. "Malcolm X: The Man and His Times" (original work published in 1969). In *Malcolm X: Justice Seeker*, edited by James B. Gwynne, pp. 39-47. New York: Steppingstones Press.

Combs, Dennis R., et al. 2006. "Perceived Racism as a Predictor of Paranoia among African Americans." *The Journal of Black Psychology* 32 (1): 87-104.

Daines, Brian. 2000. "'Ours the Sorrow, Ours the Loss': Psychoanalytic Understandings of the Role of World War I War Memorials in the Mourning Process [Electronic version]." *Psychoanalytic Studies* 2 (3): 291-308.

Denzin, Norman, and Yvonna Lincoln, eds. 1998. *Strategies of Qualitative Inquiry*. Thousand Oaks, CA: Sage Publications.

Didion, Joan. 2003. "Black Panther." In *Reporting Civil Rights. Part Two: American Journalism 1963-1973*, edited by Clayborne Carson, pp. 676-680. New York: The Library of America.

Edwards, Judith. 2005. "Before the Threshold: Destruction, Reparation and Creativity in Relation to the Depressive Position [Electronic version]." *Journal of Child Psychotherapy* 31 (3): 317-334.

Fenichel, Otto. 1943. "Mourning and Its Relation to Manic-depressive States: Melanie Klein" [Abstract]. *International Journal of Psychoanalysis* 21:125-153 (Full paper published in 1940). *Psychoanalytic Quarterly* 12:288-289. http://search.ebscohost.com/login.aspx?direct=true&db=pph&AN=PAQ.012.0288B&site=ehost-live (retrieved January 11, 2008).

Frady, Marshall. 2002. *Martin Luther King, Jr.* New York: The Penguin Group.

Freud, Sigmund. 1995. "The History of the Psychoanalytic Movement" (original work published in 1914). In *The Basic Writings of Sigmund Freud,* edited and translated by A. A. Brill, pp. 899-948. New York: Random House.

——. (1917). "Mourning and Melancholia." *Standard Edition* 14:243-258. http://search.ebscohost.com/login.aspx?direct=true&db=pph&AN=SE.014.0237A&site=ehost-live (retrieved January 17, 2007).

Fromm, Erich. 1969. *Escape from Freedom.* New York: Henry Holt and Company.

Golafshani, Nahid. 2003. "Understanding Reliability and Validity in Qualitative Research [Electronic version]." *The Qualitative Report* 8 (4): 597-607.

Gurwitsch, Aron. 1966. *Studies in Phenomenology and Psychology.* Evanston: Northwestern University Press.

Haley, Alex, and Malcolm X. 1965. *The Autobiography of Malcolm X: As Told to Alex Haley.* New York: The Random House Publishing Group.

Haley, James, ed. 2004. *Reparations for American Slavery.* San Diego: Greenhaven Press.

Heron-Scott, Gil. 1970. *Small Talk at 125th and Lenox.* Flying Dutchman Records.

Hilliard, David, with Keith and Kent Zimmerman. 2006. *Huey: Spirit of the Panther.* New York: Thunder's Mouth Press.

Hillman, James. 1983. *Healing Fiction.* Barrytown, NY: Station Hill Press.

Hinshelwood, R. D. 1991. *A Dictionary of Kleinian Thought: Second Edition.* Northvale, NJ: Jason Aronson.

Horney, Karen. 1945. *Our Inner Conflicts: A Constructive Theory of Neurosis.* New York: W.W. Norton & Company.

References

Hughes, Langston. 1990, 1959. *Selected Poems of Langston Hughes.* New York: Random House.

Hutchinson, Earl Ofari. 1990. *The Mugging of Black America.* Chicago, IL: African American Images.

Joiner, Lottie L. 2008. "Silent Pain." *The Crisis* 115 (3): 24-28.

Jones, Ernest. 1953. *The Life and Work of Sigmund Freud: Volume 1.* New York: Basic Books.

Kelley, Robin D. G. 2002. *Freedom Dreams: The Black Radical Imagination.* Boston: Beacon Press.

Klein, Melanie. 1935. "A Contribution to the Psychogenesis of Manic-Depressive States." *International Journal of Psychoanalysis* 16:145-174. http://search.ebsco host.com/ login.aspx?direct=true&db=pph&AN= IJP.016.0145A&site=ehost-live (retrieved December 19, 2007).

———. 1929. "Infantile Anxiety-Situations Reflected in a Work of Art and in the Creative Impulse." *International Journal of Psychoanalysis* 10:436-443. http:// search.ebscohost.com/login.aspx?direct=true&db= pph&AN=IJP.010.0436A&site=ehost-live (retrieved January 17, 2007).

———. 1940. "Mourning and Its Relation to Manic-Depressive States." *The International Journal of Psychoanalysis* 21:125-153.

———. 1986. "The Psychological Principles of Infant Analysis." In *The Selected Melanie Klein,* edited by Juliet Mitchell, pp. 57-68 (original work published in 1926). New York: The Free Press.

Klein, Melanie, and Joan Riviere. 1964. *Love, Hate and Reparation.* New York: W.W. Norton & Company.

Lee, Edward N., and Maurice Mandelbaum, eds. 1967. *Phenomenology and Existentialism.* Baltimore: The John Hopkins Press.

Likierman, Meira. 2001. *Melanie Klein: Her Work in Context.* New York: The Continuum International Publishing Group.

Litwack, Leon F. 1998. *Trouble in Mind: Black Southerners in the Age of Jim Crow.* New York: Alfred A. Knopf.

Luijpen, William A. 1966. *Phenomenology and Humanism.* Pittsburgh: Duquesne University Press.

Lutzky, Harriet. 1989. "Reparation and Tikkun: A Comparison of the Kleinian and Kabbalistic Concepts." *International Review of Psychoanalysis* 16:449-458. http://search.ebscohost.com/login.aspx?direct=true& db=pph&AN=IRP.016.0449A&site=ehost-live (retrieved September 27, 2009).

Major, Reginald. 1971. *A Panther Is a Black Cat.* New York: William Morrow & Company.

Mason, A. A. 1977. "Paranoid and Depressive Positions in Marital Relations." *Modern Psychoanalysis* 2 (1): 43-54. http://search. ebscohost.com/login.aspx?direct= true&db=pph&AN=MPSA.002.0043A&site=ehost-live (retrieved December 29, 2008).

Meerloo, Joost A. M. 1956. *The Rape of the Mind: The Psychology of Thought Control, Menticide, and Brainwashing.* Cleveland: The World Publishing Company.

Oates, Stephen B. 1994. *Let the Trumpet Sound: The Life of Martin Luther King, Jr.* New York: Harper Perennial.

Peery, J. Craig. 2002. "Archetype and Object: Primary Deintegration and Primary Love in Analytical Play Therapy with Young Children [Electronic version]." *Journal of Analytical Psychology* 47 (3): 407-420.

Rajiv, Sudhi. 1992. *Forms of Black Consciousness.* New York: Advent Books.

Randall, Dudley. 1968. *Cities Burning.* Detroit: Broadside Press.

References

The Random House Dictionary of the English Language (2nd ed.). 1987. New York: Random House.

Rey, J. H. 1988. "That Which Patients Bring to Analysis." *International Journal of Psychoanalysis* 69:457-470. http://search.ebscohost.com/login.aspx?direct=true&db=pph&AN=IJP.069.0457A&site=ehost-live (retrieved December 26, 2007).

Roazen, Paul. 1974. *Freud and His Followers.* New York: Da Capo Press.

Robinson, Randall. 2002. *The Reckoning: What Blacks Owe to Each Other.* New York: Dutton.

Rosenfeld, Herbert. 1959. "An Investigation into the Psychoanalytic Theory of Depression." *International Journal of Psychoanalysis* 40:105-129. http://search.ebscohost.com/login.aspx?direct=true&db=pph&AN=IJP.040. 0105A&site=ehost-live (retrieved March 29, 2008).

Sales, William W., Jr. 1994. *From Civil Rights to Black Liberation: Malcolm X and the Organization of Afro-American Unity.* Boston: South End Press.

Salzberger, Ronald P., and Mary C. Turck, eds. 2004. *Reparations for Slavery: A Reader.* New York: Rowman & Littlefield Publishers.

Sandler, Joseph, M.D. 2003. "On Attachment to Internal Objects [Electronic version]." *Psychoanalytic Inquiry* 23 (1): 12-26.

Sayre, Nora. 2003. "Black Panthers and White Radicals: September-November 1970 / The Revolutionary People's Constitutional Convention." In *Reporting Civil Rights. Part Two: American Journalism 1963-1973,* edited by Clayborne Carson, pp. 847-856. New York: The Library of America.

Schimmel, Paul. 1998. "Medicine and the Manic Defense [Electronic version]." *Australian & New Zealand Journal of Psychiatry* 32 (3): 392-397.

Segal, Hanna. 1964. *Introduction to the Work of Melanie Klein.* New York: Basic Books Publishing Co.

Sloan, Cle "Bone" (Director and Co-Producer). 2005. *Bastards of the Party* [Motion picture]. USA: Fuqua Films.

Solomon, H. 1991. "Archetypal Psychology and Object Relations Theory: History and Commonalities [Electronic version]." *Journal of Analytical Psychology* 36 (3): 307-329.

St. Clair, Michael. 2000. *Object Relations and Self Psychology: An Introduction* (3rd ed.). Canada: Wadsworth.

Steiner, John. 1992. "The Equilibrium Between the Paranoid-Schizoid and the Depressive Positions." *The New Library of Psychoanalysis* 14:46-58. http://search. ebscohost.com/login.aspx?direct= true&db=pph& AN=NLP.014.0046A&site=ehost-live (retrieved December 29, 2008).

Stern, Sol. 2003. "The Call of the Black Panthers." In *Reporting Civil Rights. Part Two: American Journalism 1963-1973,* edited by Clayborne Carson, pp. 624-636. New York: The Library of America.

Stewart, David, and Algis Mickunas. 1974. *Exploring Phenomenology.* Chicago: American Library Association.

Terrill, Robert E. 2004. *Malcolm X: Inventing Radical Judgment.* East Lansing: Michigan State University Press.

Thernstrom, Stephan, and Abigail Thernstrom. 2000. "King's Rise to Prominence in Montgomery." In *Martin Luther King, Jr.,* edited by Thomas Siebold, pp. 117-125. San Diego: Greenhaven Press.

Torpey, John. 2006. *Making Whole What Has Been Smashed: On Reparations Politics.* Cambridge, MA: Harvard University Press.

References

Vernell, Marjorie. 2000. *Leaders of Black Civil Rights.* San Diego: Lucent Books.

Webster's New Collegiate Dictionary. 1980. Springfield, MA: G. & C. Merriam Co.

West, Cornel. 1993. *Race Matters.* Boston: Beacon Press.

Wilson, Amos N. 1991. *Understanding Black Adolescent Male Violence: Its Prevention and Remediation.* New York: Afrikan World Infosystems.

Winbush, Raymond A. 2003. *Should America Pay? Slavery and the Raging Debate on Reparations.* New York: HarperCollins Publishers.

Wood, Joe, ed. 1992. *Malcolm X: In Our Own Image.* New York: St. Martin's Press.

Wormser, Richard. 2003. *The Rise and Fall of Jim Crow.* New York: St. Martin's Press.

Notes

Notes

Notes

Notes

Notes

Notes

Notes